Spiritual and Broke

*How to Stop Struggling with Money
and Live Your Purpose*

JENNIFER NOEL TAYLOR

UNION SQUARE
PUBLISHING

Published by
Union Square Publishing
301 E. 57th Street, 4th floor
New York, NY 10022
www.unionsquarepublishing.com

Manufactured in the United States of America, or in the United Kingdom when distributed elsewhere.

Taylor, Jennifer
   Spiritual and Broke: How to Stop Struggling with Money and Live Your Purpose
   LCCN: 2018965834
   ISBN: 978-1-946928-22-1
   eBook: 978-1-946928-23-8

Cover design by: Joe Potter and Patrick Feld
Copyediting and interior design by: Claudia Volkman

www.jennifernoeltaylor.com
www.quantumtouch.com

They say, "Do what you love,
and the money will come."
So, today I ate an entire bar of
dark chocolate, snuggled with a kitten,
and curled up in bed with my favorite book.
Now I wait . . .

TABLE OF CONTENTS

Foreword   1
Are You Spiritual and Broke?   3
Leap of Faith   19
Secret Shame   39
Police Car Epiphany   57
The Law of Attraction Revisited   69
Selective Ownership   87
The Essential Shift   107
Why Budgets Fail   119
Divine Guidance   131
The Magic of Simplicity   159
Am I Worthy?   177
Spiritual and Abundant   199
Acknowledgments   207
About the Author   209

They say that love is more important than money,
but have you ever tried to pay your bills with a hug?
NISHAN PANWAR

FOREWORD

Are You Spiritual and Broke?

Having worked in the field of energy medicine for over thirty years, as I see it, if you are not thriving, there are three primary arenas of your life which may need healing: your health, your relationships, and your wallet. All three arenas are clear expressions of your emotional and spiritual health. So many people I've known experience a deep connection to their spirituality, yet they struggle financially.

If you can relate to how this feels, suffer no more. There is hope. Welcome to *Spiritual and Broke*.

Before I dive into this book, let me tell you that I've known Jennifer Taylor for over sixteen years as a best friend and business partner, and I have had the opportunity to closely observe her growth and transformation. She is the real deal—honest, sincere, vulnerable. And most importantly, she's fully living the truths she presents in this book. (I have absolutely no patience for those who cannot exemplify what they teach.)

The cliché of "do what you love and the money will follow" is tragically and severely oversimplified, and it is not a solution to many complex issues. If you've been spiritual and broke, you probably already know this far too well.

We tend to see patterns occurring again and again in our lives, and hopefully sooner or later we realize that these patterns are of our own making. It is as if events that repeat themselves have our own fingerprints all over them. If you choose to identify yourself as a victim, then put this book back on the shelf; it is not for you. But if you suspect that you hold the keys to change, read on!

Spiritual and Broke can help you understand why "good" people sometimes attract tragedies. For many, the pain of a tragedy serves as a monumental fuel for change. While never appreciated in the moment, you may learn to discover how these experiences can be absolutely necessary. For sometimes, it takes a "dark miracle" to shake up the old patterns in order to inspire spectacular growth.

So, congratulations for finding this book. Now is your time to thrive!

—Richard Gordon, author and
founder of Quantum-Touch

ARE YOU SPIRITUAL AND BROKE?

*The only exercise I've done this month
is running out of money.*

EARL WILSON

The "Aha!" Moment

Some people have "Aha!" moments,
I just have "Oh seriously???" moments.

AUTHOR UNKNOWN

Have you ever had a moment in your life that was so shocking, so horrible, and yet appeared so absurdly random that you were compelled to wonder:

"How the heck did I end up here?"

I had that exact moment at 6:00 a.m. one crisp fall morning in Venice, California. The sun was just peeking out over the eastern horizon, painting the sky with a rich palette of reds, oranges, and yellows. Enhanced by a thick, noxious, and ever-present layer of infamous LA smog, the dazzling colors illuminated the city with breathtaking splendor. As the new day dawned, I watched this glorious sunrise from a perverse, unfamiliar, creepy, and totally unthinkable place . . .

The back of a police car.

What?

Yes, that's right! Sadly, I *wasn't* enjoying this spectacular sunrise from a comfy sectional while savoring a cup of my favorite French press coffee. Nor was I heading out for a peaceful morning run or catering to the dietary whims of a finicky pet cat. Instead I was anxiously sitting in the back seat of a police car, reflecting upon the ugly sequence of events that had led up to this horrifying situation.

Many leaders, teachers, saints, and even the Merriam-Webster dictionary refer to an experience like this as an

5

"Aha!" moment: "a moment of sudden realization, inspiration, or insight." It is often characterized by a sense that time is "standing still." In a state of shock, we watch our life unfold from a vantage point somewhere outside our body. This surreal moment forces us to reconstruct our very essence on the spot; we know, without a doubt, that we will never be the same person we once were.

In my case, this "Aha!" moment acted as a profound catalyst for change—an opportunity to make a significant "course correction" in my life.

Looking back, I was *way* overdue for a major shift.

Negative Net Worth

Before my "Aha!" moment, I had been feeling incredibly stuck; I was perpetually spinning my wheels in a pit of fathomless desperation. My life had become a constant, never-ending, painful, and depressing struggle with money.

How did I, an intelligent, level-headed, college-educated, and supposedly savvy woman, end up incredibly broke? More specifically, how did I end up with no money, copious amounts of debt, and no savings?

Let me describe my previously pitiful state of financial affairs . . .

First of all, my checking account was on life support; my balance always hovered well below the arbitrary "minimum daily balance," prompting the bank to levy a significant (and annoying!) monthly fee.

Second, I had accumulated $35,000 of credit card debt, and the *interest alone* was significantly higher than my car payment and utility bills combined. To add insult to injury, oftentimes the finance charge would push my card over the limit, prompting the bank to assess yet another irritating fee. Just keeping my balance under the limit (let alone paying it off) proved to be more difficult than persuading a playful kitten to stop climbing the curtains!

Third, in addition to my credit card debt, whimsical bank fees, and unfathomable interest charges, I also owed $100,000 on a business line of credit. Now, one might argue that a commercial loan is not necessarily a bad thing, *if* it eventually generates a return on investment. However, in my case, this loan wasn't funding any sort of business growth. Instead, it was the only lifeboat keeping my business afloat. Without it, I would have been forced to close the doors.

Finally, to cap it all off, I had absolutely zero savings. I was in no position to handle unanticipated expenses, such as a car repair, a sudden dip in business, a visit to the dentist, a plumbing emergency, or even the adoption of a kitten! And forget about having enough money saved for a down payment on a house or a trip to see the family. Like many people, I was living paycheck to paycheck.

Now don't get me wrong, I enjoyed what *appeared* to be a wonderfully abundant lifestyle. However, my copacetic way of life was *only* possible because I was highly skilled at *borrowing* money! For example, I had an "interest only" mortgage on my dream home in Hawaii. Unfortunately, as you may know, this type of loan behaves like a ticking time bomb; once the "interest only" period expires, the mortgage payment increases substantially! Hence, I had a beautiful house I couldn't afford (long-term.) I also made sizeable monthly payments on a bright, shiny, "fire engine red" Mazda Miata convertible, which I absolutely loved, especially on sunny days! Unfortunately, my favorite toy also added an additional $30,000 to my total debt.

Furthermore, I frequently splurged on makeup, sparkly shoes, a personal trainer, new clothes, and high-end linen throw pillows—all of which was possible thanks to MasterCard.

Taking the thirty thousand-foot view of my financial portfolio, I had:

- a $100,000 business loan
- $35,000 of credit card debt
- a mortgage I couldn't afford
- an auto loan
- zero savings

Sadly, I wasn't just broke; I was *beyond broke*! I actually needed to *raise* money just to bring my net worth to *zero*. Regrettably, my life of costly creature comforts came with a steep emotional price tag as well—I constantly felt anxious and stressed about money (or more specifically, the lack thereof!)

Follow Your Heart and the Money Will Come?

All of my financial troubles began when I quit my "real job" to follow my heart. I may have been naïve, but at that time, I was under the impression that if I did what I loved, the money would follow. However, much to my dismay, the money never came! Sadly, my beloved ideology didn't work for me.

Not at all!

Here's what really happened . . .

Previously, I worked as a software developer, and while I wasn't in love with my job, I appreciated the reliable paycheck and benefits that came with it. Even though I was financially solvent, I was *emotionally bankrupt.* I felt disillusioned by my work and often wondered, "Is this all there is?" I believe we are all put on earth to do something meaningful, and for me, it was *not* writing software in a cold, lonely cubicle, day in and day out!

Everything changed when I attended a lecture by Richard Gordon, the founder of an energy healing company called Quantum-Touch®. As you may know, energy healing is a form of alternative medicine based on channeling healing energy to facilitate physical, emotional, and spiritual well-being. During his talk, I fell in love with Richard and his mission to teach energy healing all over the world. And as we all know, falling in love can inspire us do insanely wonderful things! Just two months after we met, I threw all caution to the wind, quit my "real job," and moved in with him.

Unfortunately, as I soon discovered, Quantum-Touch was on the verge of going out of business. In fact, shortly after I settled in with Richard, the current CEO of Quantum-Touch decided to quit! Prompted by an uncertain future, she wanted to find a "real job"—a secure position at a profitable and stable company. Ironically, she wanted the exact same type of job *I had just left*. And who could blame her? I certainly understood her desire to jump off a sinking ship! Hence, she invited me to take over her position, and that's how I became the CEO (or "Chief Magical Officer," as I like say) of Quantum-Touch.

Despite the bleak state of the company, I loved my new role! I felt extremely passionate about the paradigm behind energy medicine. Although conventional medicine views the body as physical matter, Quantum-Touch sees the body as consciousness, information, and energy, all of which can be dramatically influenced by our love and compassion. In other words, we all have an incredible ability to heal ourselves using the power of love. I longed to share this inspiring message with the world, and I saw Quantum-Touch as my vehicle to do just that!

Regrettably, though, as much as I loved living my purpose, working with Quantum-Touch *did not* create the financial abundance that I was so eagerly anticipating. In fact, it created just the opposite—lots of debt and stress around money. We were always teetering on the edge of going out of business, and I found myself acquiring debt faster than a hyper hamster running in his wheel. Pondering my negative net worth, I couldn't help but wonder:

What went so horribly wrong?

How did I end up spiritual and broke?

Love Versus Money?

Whenever I thought about how to fix my negative net worth, it seemed like my only options were either terribly disheartening or utterly impossible. I felt completely stuck.

I considered going back to the "real world" and getting a normal job. On the upside, I would once again enjoy a nice steady paycheck, and perhaps I could slowly dig myself out of my massive and unfathomable financial hole. This idea seemed extremely tempting at times, yet in my heart I knew I couldn't do it. I would be going back to feeling unfulfilled, depressed, and miserable at my job. What sense would that make? I knew I had a unique purpose on the planet, and no matter how I framed it, getting a "real job" would be selling out; I would no longer be following my heart. *I would be sacrificing my soul for money.*

Cutting back on my spending seemed like an obvious solution, but that didn't work either! Every time I tried to lower my expenses, I felt like I was following a dangerous and ill-advised crash diet, with unhappy and even perilous consequences. For example, organic food is significantly more expensive than fast food, yet I didn't want to stop eating healthy *just* to save money. Scrimping on transportation was equally problematic; instead of keeping my car as long as possible, I always traded it in prematurely because I didn't want to risk breaking down. And like many healers, I am extremely sensitive to the energy of my environment, so instead of renting a cheap, noisy apartment, I spent a lot of money on a quiet, nurturing place to live. Hence, no matter how I looked at it, *saving money meant sacrificing my health, security, and happiness.*

To avoid any of these tough decisions, I rationalized my debt, telling myself it was inconsequential because *someday* my ship would come in. Sooner or later, the Universe would *reward* me for all my hard work and eventually I would receive the abundance I had so greatly *earned* and *deserved.* I constantly entertained fantasies of going to the bank and proudly writing a substantial check to pay off all my debt. (And then I would open one of those special checking accounts for people with lots of money.) I dreamed about the day my money worries would be a distant memory.

Essentially, I was treating my debt as a way to *buy time* while I waited for the Universe to pay me my due. After all, the Universe *should* reward us for having the courage to follow our heart and share our love with the world . . .

Right?

However, there was a big problem with my rationale: *the*

money never came! Year after year, nothing changed. I was working so hard to help others, yet I felt like a *victim*—a *martyr* for my cause. I talked about the power of love, yet behind closed doors, I was angry at God. I felt incredibly betrayed by the Universe.

Furthermore, I was not alone in my financial despair. As the old saying goes, "Misery loves company!" Just like me, many of my friends and colleagues were living their purpose, yet felt frustrated, angry, and disappointed by their complete and utter failure to make ends meet. Believe it or not, I actually met life coaches who were living out of their cars or "couch surfing," unable to afford a place to live. I knew other business owners who maxed out their credit cards to fund their mission and, like me, had no savings to handle a downturn in sales or an emergency expense. Worst of all, despite my own financial problems, I sometimes loaned money to friends who were also spiritual and broke. Sadly, these loans typically turned into unintended "gifts."

Overall, it just didn't seem fair that so many sincere, heart-centered entrepreneurs constantly struggle with money. Why are so many beautiful, amazing people living their purpose, yet extremely stressed about taking care of their family, loved ones, and employees?

Why?

What is the Universe trying to tell us?

Should we stop trying to follow our heart?

Do we have to choose between love and money?

Police Car Epiphany

As bestselling author H. Jackson Brown Jr. observed, "Every great achievement was once considered impossible." Like many people living paycheck to paycheck, I felt trapped in an impossible cycle of debt. I began to believe that I would *never* achieve financial inner peace, that I would *never* get out of debt, and that I would *always* remain hopelessly spiritual and broke. I felt like I was doomed forever, until I had my "Aha!" moment in the back of that police car. Later I will share the gory details of *exactly* how I ended up there—the one place I thought I would *never* be! As I watched a glorious sunrise illuminate one of the darkest moments in my life, I experienced an epiphany that radically altered my worldview. I finally understood why I was struggling with my finances (and other aspects of my life as well.) My "police car epiphany" was the catalyst I so desperately needed to turn my finances around.

Now, I am debt-free and no longer burdened by $135,000 of unsecured financial baggage. I have established a real savings account, instead of using my credit card as the "emergency fund." I have more than enough money saved for car repairs, plumbing leaks, fancy cat toys, a new sectional, a vacation, or even a down payment on a house! I consistently save money each month. My net worth has gone from insanely negative to comfortably positive. I no longer constantly agonize about running out of money.

More importantly, I turned my finances around *without any feelings of deprivation or sacrificing my well-being.* I never felt like I was embarking on some irritating, misguided, and unsustainable financial diet.

And believe me, if I can do it, anyone can!

Financial Alignment

Now, let me clarify something: this book is *not* about making lots and lots of money! As we all know, it's possible to make oodles of money and *still be broke*! Some people earn millions a year, yet they have mounds of debt and spend every penny they make. Hence, this goes to show that turning our finances around has very little to do with how much money we *actually make.* Furthermore, this book is *not* about forcing ourselves to follow a frugal lifestyle either. For many of us, trying to sacrifice our happiness and well-being to save money is like going on a painful and extreme crash diet; it just doesn't work long-term.

Instead, this book is a guide to what I refer to as "financial alignment"—a harmonious *co-existence* between our heart and our money. In a state of financial alignment, we *naturally* (and painlessly!) spend less than we earn *while* we are living our purpose. We joyfully pursue our true calling in life without constantly worrying about how to make ends meet. We don't have to sacrifice our soul to make money or sacrifice our finances to follow our heart. (Nor do we have to sacrifice our trips to the spa!)

And here's my favorite part about financial alignment: it supports our true calling by *allowing us to fund it*.

It empowers us to do what we love!

So, what does financial alignment look like?

First of all, we are doing what we *love*. We don't just show up at work as an aloof, burned-out drone for the sole purpose of collecting a paycheck. Instead, we are passionate about what we do. We are helping others, and we know, *without a doubt*, that we are fulfilling our true purpose.

Second, we have no debt. This means no credit card debt, no car loans, no bank loans, and no money owed to friends and family. The only exception to this is debt that actually builds wealth, such as an affordable (non-interest only) mortgage. At the risk of stating the obvious, debt is not only a financial burden, it's a heavy emotional burden as well. It can weigh down our creative spirit, curtail our inspiration, and even thwart our mission in life. Not to mention, the interest alone can feel insurmountable and downright depressing!

Third, we *happily and easily* live below our means. After all our monthly expenses are paid, we have *money to spare*. Please note, I said "happily" live below our means because I believe that anyone can drastically cut their expenses if they are willing to endure enough pain and suffering. Anyone can pitch a tent in the woods, ride a bike in the snow, and eat ramen noodles as their only source of sustenance. This book, however, is about financial and emotional *abundance*, not deprivation. We can live below our means and *still* have money left over to enjoy the little luxuries in life such as dinners out, organic cat food, a pedicure, skydiving, or whatever makes our heart sing.

Finally, we have a decent-sized savings account, ideally with at least one year of expenses saved. It's very tempting to think of a credit card as the "fund for emergencies," yet relying on credit is the mentality that creates debt in the first place! Also, because we are *cheerfully* living below our means, we consistently and *painlessly* save money, month after month.

In this book, I describe everything I did, step-by-step, to create financial alignment—*without* feeling deprived, overworked, or overwhelmed. My financial turnaround was possible *only because I didn't feel like I was suffering in the process.* I never felt imprisoned by an unrealistic and torturous budget. Nor did I force myself to earn more money by working ridiculously long hours or getting a second job.

Here's the bottom line: We can turn our finances around, *right here, right now,* regardless of our current situation. We don't need to wait until we have more money or a better job. In fact, we don't need to wait for anything or anyone; there's no need to wait for our spouse to change, or for our children to move out, or for someone to die, or for an act of God. We *all* have the power, *right now,* to create *more than enough* money to follow our heart, live our purpose, and enjoy the life of our dreams...

Or at least pay the rent on time!

When your life is on course with its purpose,
you are your most powerful.
OPRAH WINFREY

LEAP OF FAITH

"It's impossible," said Pride.
"It's risky," said Experience.
"It's pointless," said Reason.
"Give it a try," whispered the HEART.

AUTHOR UNKNOWN

"Ready . . . Hep!"

*"Anything I've ever done that ultimately was worthwhile
initially scared me to death."*
BETTY BENDER

September 2, 2011

I was a bundle of nerves standing on a tiny rectangular platform, twenty-five feet in the air. It was an especially hot day at the Los Angeles County Fair, and the extreme heat combined with my intense fear was a really, really bad combination. My normally shy persona was wrestling with my current predicament: I was dressed in a glittery purple costume, getting ready to perform a nerve-wracking circus act high above a very large crowd. Honestly, I'm not sure which was worse: my fear of heights, the flamboyant costume, or my performance anxiety!

I had recently said yes to my dream come true, a once-in-a-lifetime opportunity to perform on the high-flying trapeze! Remember going to the circus and watching the flying trapeze? Few things compare to the magical awesomeness of seeing a troupe of flyers perform death-defying aerial feats, high above the crowd. The most dramatic part of the flying trapeze is the moment when the flyer is caught (hopefully!) by another acrobat (the catcher) who is swinging upside down on a separate "catch bar." The timing for all of this to happen is extremely precise, so the catcher will yell "Hep!" when it's time for the flyer to take off. If the flyer doesn't jump exactly on cue, he or

21

she will most likely miss the catch and plummet to the net. The flying trapeze *literally* takes a leap of faith!

In my case, the exhilaration of flying through the air always went hand in hand with an equally intense feeling of fear. Even after five years of training, I was still a nervous wreck as I stood on the platform, preparing to perform my trick for the audience. Anxiously leaning out over the ledge, I reached out with my overly sweaty right hand and grabbed the fly bar. Seconds seemed to stretch into minutes as I waited for the catcher to give me my cue to jump. Finally, I heard a barely audible "Hep" over the loud music. I immediately swung the fly bar up to me and took off. Doing my best to ignore my internal panic, the excessive heat, and the lively audience, I performed my trick and prayed. Much to my relief, the catcher grabbed my forearms, as my "leap of faith" was met by his competent hands.

Speaking of fear, swinging on the flying trapeze wasn't the first time I had dabbled with a death-defying and scary leap of faith. Nine years before I joined the circus, I did something far more precarious—I left a stable, well-paying job and leaped into the unknown. I quit my job as a software developer, moved in with Richard, a man I barely knew, and, despite having no background in business, accepted an offer to become CEO of Quantum-Touch. I followed my heart, praying that I would somehow be caught by the competent hands of a benevolent Universe.

Did I land safely?

Well, here's my story . . .

A "Bad Case of the Mondays"

In 1996 I graduated with a degree in computer science from California Polytechnic State University in San Luis Obispo, California. The degree served as a minor distraction from the college parties, philosophy classes, friends, food, and fun. Hence, I was not prepared for the level of depression and boredom that set in fairly quickly after I graduated. After investing so much time, energy, and (my parent's) money into my degree, I found myself feeling tremendously disappointed as I embarked on my new career as a software engineer.

After graduation, I accepted a job offer from a large corporation in San Diego, California. Although many people feel excited when they start a new career, I dreaded my job. I lived for the weekend. In fact, one might say I suffered from "a bad case of the Mondays"—a gloomy sense of foreboding at the beginning of the workweek. When Sunday evening rolled around, I always felt depressed and resentful knowing I had to work the next day. I was basically going to work *just to collect a paycheck*.

Why was I so miserable?

First of all, I detested the work environment in general. For eight hours a day, I lived in a cubicle: a special workspace that expertly blocked my view of the outside world. Yet this square marvel of engineering failed to mask even subtle noises (or smells!) from other co-workers. Also, I could have sworn that the office thermostat only had one setting: freezing-cold! My cubicle always felt like the inside of a meat locker, basically leaving me uncomfortable all day, every day.

Second, my job was more tedious than watching a Saguaro grow in a desert. I spent most of my time writing copious amounts of very detailed, uninspiring, mind-numbing, and monotonous lines of code. The lackluster work combined with my incredibly apathetic attitude prompted me to question my perception of time. Could time actually *travel backward* inside my arctic prison? Every minute felt like an eternity. Yet, despite my nonchalance, I was fairly competent at what I did. Therefore, I always ran out of work, leaving me with nothing to do other than occupy my desk and *pretend* to work until the end of the day. At *precisely* 5:00 p.m., I would hastily vacate my frigid office, cherishing my few precious hours of freedom until the next workday.

Third, I was scared for my future self. I have a very distinct memory of attending a company awards ceremony, where I watched *in awe* as an employee received an award for thirty years of service. *How could someone endure the same job, day in and day out, for so long?* I wondered. I couldn't help but notice that he looked very weary, as though his job had taken an immense toll on his joy for life. I felt terrified that I, too, would end up as a burned-out, miserable person. I couldn't imagine wasting the best years of my life feeling so lifeless and unfulfilled, just so I could scrape together enough money for rent and food.

Fourth, I spent the majority of my time alone, trapped in my glacial penitentiary, staring at a computer. Consequently, I always felt extremely isolated and lonely throughout the workday. My lack of social contact steadily chipped away at my well-being, adding to my overall sense of disillusionment.

As an attempt to find some relief from my mundane and troubled existence, I changed jobs multiple times. After just one year, I quit my job in San Diego and accepted a position in Central California. Over the next four years, I worked for two different companies. Yet none of these changes helped me overcome my restlessness and alienation. Even landing a job in Maui, Hawaii, (my dream location!) didn't soothe my troubled soul. In a nutshell, I hated my job.

Well, I think I've made my point.

By the way, if one of my former employers is reading this book, my aversion to work had nothing to do with you or the people I worked with! Overall, I just felt deeply depressed by the prospect of writing software in a cold and lonely office *for the rest of my life.* Although I tried to put on a happy face and make the best of it, I still had this nagging feeling that I was *supposed to be doing something else.* Every day, as I dragged myself to work, I constantly begged the Universe for some direction:

Please, please, please show me my purpose in life.

Haven't I suffered enough?

I knew without a doubt that I *wasn't* living my true

calling, but I had absolutely no clue how to actually *find* my purpose. Although I was making a very nice salary, the money alone wasn't enough for me. I felt like my spirit was dying. I *desperately* needed some answers because I knew couldn't continue much longer.

As the old saying goes, "God works in mysterious ways." Perhaps the Universe grew weary of my constant begging and pleading, because, little did I know, my purpose was about to find me.

Ask and You Shall Receive

As author and theologian Frederick Buechner wrote, "Purpose is the place where your deep gladness meets the world's needs." I love this definition of "purpose" because it implies that pursuing our true calling is analogous to living the life of our dreams.

How cool is that!

Somehow, many of us have adopted idea that helping others means sacrificing a part of our selves, taking a vow of poverty, or replacing our sparkly Manolo Blahnik satin heels with old, ugly, smelly tennis shoes. However, living our purpose is exactly the opposite! It's not meant to be a miserable life full of pain, suffering, poverty, and sacrifice. Rather, it's the intersection between our *greatest joy* and *highest service* to the world.

The Universe is constantly nudging us to live our purpose. Oftentimes it may reveal our true calling by "speaking" to us through our intuition, dreams, a sense of knowing, actual events in our lives, or, that "still small voice of the heart." (We'll talk a lot about the still small voice and how to hear it later on.) In my case, the Universe unveiled my life purpose in a very unexpected yet miraculous way.

Like many journeys of self-discovery, mine originated from a place of intense discontent. Spending most of my workday in solitary confinement, I desperately craved the loving touch of another person or even just the comfort of mingling with others. So, as an attempt to counteract this painful and depressing social isolation, I enrolled in massage school after work.

During the yearlong course, I studied various healing modalities, including Shiatsu, energy healing, Hawaiian Lomi Lomi, and deep tissue massage. Although I enjoyed all of the various bodywork techniques, one technique in particular really stood out: I fell head-over-heals in love with energy healing!

Energy healing is a hands-on healing technique that balances the flow of energy in the body. The practitioner channels energy—also known as "Qi," "Prana," or "life force energy"—to facilitate the healing process. Up until I attended massage school, I had no clue that energy healing even existed. However, once I discovered it, I turned into a die-hard energy fanatic! I spent hours playing with the Qi coming from my hands, utterly fascinated by this mysterious energetic force. I also started to feel the life force energy emanating from others, and I could even see auras around some people. I knew instinctively that energy healing had the potential to create miracles!

Shortly after I discovered my love for energy healing, something rather bizarre happened: the Universe "spoke" to me. To clarify, I didn't hear a loud, booming voice from the heavens, complete with doves and trumpets. I didn't see a heavenly host of angels, joyfully signing hallelujah as they proudly handed me an inscribed tablet, clearly outlining the reason for my existence. Instead, I simply received a very distinct, intuitive message about my true calling in life. My still small voice said:

"Energy healing is your life purpose."

My response?

I concluded that the Universe clearly had absolutely no clue what it was talking about! First of all, up until then, I hadn't had much experience with the "still small voice." I couldn't help but wonder if it was just my imagination. Did I really have a purpose or would I always be an insignificant cog in the wheel of life? Second, in the year 2002, energy healing was this seemingly bizarre fringe idea very few people believed in. And third, how could I possibly *make a living* doing energy healing? The whole idea seemed absurd, irrational, and impractical. Yet, despite my misgivings, I still loved the idea of doing healing work full-time.

Shortly after the Universe apparently informed me of my life purpose, I received yet another curious message. This time it happened when I attended a lecture about a particular modality of energy healing called Quantum-Touch. Richard Gordon, the founder of Quantum-Touch, gave the talk and offered free energy healing demonstrations. During the lecture, I found myself deeply resonating with his heartfelt desire to help people recognize the value and impact of their love. He wanted to change the world, and I felt the same way! Although I didn't know it at the time, I had just met the man that would completely turn my life upside down.

Throughout his lecture, I felt an overwhelming sense that I was supposed to become involved with Quantum-Touch. My still small voice had spoken again, and now I was even more convinced that the Universe was totally nuts. The whole idea seemed wackier than collecting one hundred rubber ducks, scattering them in the bathtub, and then arranging them in tactical formation! First of all, his company was in California, and I lived on Maui. Second, he didn't have any job openings that I was aware of. And third, he was a complete stranger. Was I just supposed to walk up to him and say, "By the way, the Universe told me that I am destined to work with your company?"

Yet again, despite my apprehension, I felt inspired and intrigued by the guidance I heard from that still small voice within me.

Leap of Faith or Stupid Decision?

I'm quitting to pursue my dream of not working here.
AUTHOR UNKNOWN

When Richard left Maui after his lecture, I assumed I would never hear from him again. After all, I reasoned, he was a "famous" energy healing guru and best-selling author! He had a very full schedule traveling around the world, giving lectures, managing his business, and teaching workshops. Why would he want to stay in touch with an insignificant, nerdy, and socially inept software engineer on Maui? Clearly, I had some self-esteem issues! (We'll discuss the relationship between self-worth and finances later on as well.)

Given my acute feelings of self-deprecation, you can imagine my surprise when Richard called me a few days later. He invited me to attend his upcoming Quantum-Touch workshop in Honolulu, and of course, I was excited to go. Although Richard was busy teaching, we spent as much time together we could. We wandered around Chinatown, got together for lunch, and talked into the wee hours of the morning. I fell in love with Richard's heartfelt desire to help humanity, his quirky sense of humor, and his childlike fascination with the wonders of energy healing. I had to admit, connecting with Richard felt like coming home.

After this wonderful and magical weekend, I felt more depressed than ever at my job. My isolation and lack of purpose now stood in stark contrast to the deeply fulfilling connection I experienced with Richard in Honolulu. Although he called me every day, I felt uncertain whether or not I would ever see him again. He was traveling around the world, and I didn't have the luxury to join him. (Due to the fact that I hated my job, I never managed to accrue much vacation time.)

I don't remember exactly how it happened, but during one of our phone calls, Richard and I did something totally ludicrous: we decided to move in together! Although we had barely spent any time together, we both figured, "Why not?"

Why not throw all caution to the wind and take a leap of faith?

It seemed like a great idea at the time. In my case, I felt so incredibly depressed with my life, I reckoned I really had nothing to lose. (Richard later told me he felt the same way.)

When moving day came, I felt both excitement and trepidation as I boarded a plane to Santa Cruz, California. I had just quit a secure job with a steady paycheck to act upon the seemingly absurd musings of my inner voice.

Was I crazy?

Who in their right mind quits a cushy job on Maui with a large paycheck and benefits? Who moves in with someone they barely know? Yet, despite my apparent "leap of irrationality," I felt incredibly happy!

I had finally followed my heart.

As a witness to my bizarre newfound life direction, my mom also questioned the mental health of her normally level-headed daughter. "Are you sure you know what you are doing?" she asked when I called her from Santa Cruz. She continued, "Any plans to get a job?" The truth is, I really didn't have a plan! I spent all my time hanging out with Richard and had no idea where my seemingly ill-advised leap of faith would lead.

Once I arrived in Santa Cruz, I discovered that Quantum-Touch was on the brink of going out of business. Richard was feeling burned out from all of the travel and decided to take a much-needed break from being on the road 24/7. Unfortunately, when he did, the revenue in the company almost fell to zero. Consequently, the lack of income sent the current CEO of Quantum-Touch into a state of panic. Since Quantum-Touch appeared to be sinking faster than the ill-fated Titanic, she decided to jump ship and find a more secure job. Honestly, I couldn't blame her.

Before the CEO left, she called me and asked if I would like to take over her position, and I said yes. At the time, though, I didn't understand exactly what I was agreeing to. I had no background in customer service, no training in accounting, and no experience running a business. I didn't even know how to properly answer a customer phone call. I felt both totally exhilarated and completely terrified. Did I have what it takes to be a CEO? Would I regret leaving my secure job behind? Would my new job work out financially? Would Richard and I stay together?

How do we tell the difference between a leap of faith and a stupid decision?

Fear

Sometimes your only available transportation is a leap of faith.
MARGARET SHEPARD

Let's face it, a leap of faith can be scary! If we want arrive at the destination of our dreams, a leap of faith may be the only method of transportation that actually takes us there. Often, achieving what we really want in life requires us to step outside of our comfort zone and take a risk. Yet it's only natural to get cold feet when we're standing on the edge of a cliff!

How do we know that the potential upside is worth the risk?

The problem is, we don't! Oftentimes fear prevents us from taking a risk. As the incredibly successful filmmaker James Cameron said, "There are many talented people who haven't fulfilled their dreams because there were too cautious and were unwilling to make the leap of faith." And honestly, who could blame us? Who could fault us for simply being cautious? After all, a leap of faith requires us to have faith, take a risk, and put our trust in the unknown.

How scary is that?

Perhaps, we could take some comfort in the words of author Katrina Mayer: "A leap of faith is only scary until you land." However, as much as I appreciate the sentiment, I can't help but wonder, "How do we *know* we will land safely?"

Or even land at all?

It's no wonder our fear gets in the way!

It's much safer to sit on the couch than to fly through the air like some maniac, relying on precise timing of someone who is hanging upside down and swinging from a bar! Likewise, it seems much easier to tolerate a boring job, rather than sacrifice our security, take a risk, and do what we love.

Believe me, I'm no stranger to fear! Whether I was flying through the air or taking a leap of faith in "real life," fear always tended to rear its ugly head. With just a few searing words, it had the power to curtail my enthusiasm, send me into a tailspin of despair, or even dissuade me from following my heart at all. It taunted me like a sickly-sweet powdered donut; I knew it wasn't good for me, yet I couldn't resist the urge to take "just one bite." And one bite always led to another . . . and another. I resented my fear, viewing it as a sign of weakness. Why couldn't I resist the fleeting allure of the frightened voice in my head? I constantly admonished myself for even having the fear in the first place!

Even after five years of practicing the flying trapeze, I simply could *not* overcome my fear of heights. Everyone else seemed so fearless and brave. *So why couldn't I move past this fear?* I would try in vain to resist my fear, judge my fear, deny my fear, or overcome my fear. Yet the harder I worked to push it away, the more the fear would remain, like a persistent hungry kitten begging for food. It reminded me of the expression, "What we resist, persists."

My relationship with fear completely changed after a few words of wisdom from one of my trapeze instructors. He was an accomplished trapeze artist and had performed as a catcher at the Ringling Brothers Circus. His astute words have always stuck in my mind:

The goal isn't to eliminate the fear,
but to be operational with the fear present.

What a relief!

I wasn't the only person who struggled with fear. Even the catcher for the "Greatest Show on Earth" felt anxious from time to time! I finally realized that fear isn't a character flaw or something we need to "conquer." We don't need to endlessly berate ourselves if we're afraid to take a leap of faith.

Instead, we can make friends with our fear.

We can love our fear.

We can invite it to come along for the ride. However, at no point is our fear permitted to drive or navigate! (It's only allowed to sit in the back seat, passively eating potato chips.) We can embrace our fear *without* allowing it to make decisions for us. If fear happens to take over the wheel, this simply means that it's time to go back to *why* we feel compelled to take the leap in the first place. In my case, I was so inspired by energy healing that I *had* to take a leap of faith, no matter what. I came to the realize that a leap of faith is *never* a stupid decision if it's based on love.

In fact, with enough love, the fear will completely dissolve. Love is always more powerful than fear.

Just as light dissolves darkness, love dissolves fear.
AUTHOR UNKNOWN

Life After the Leap

The woods are lovely, dark, and deep,
But I have promises to keep,
And miles to go before I sleep,
And miles to go before I sleep.
ROBERT FROST

My great love for the flying trapeze often competed with my intense feelings of frustration and irritation, especially while practicing one painstaking skill in particular: "the return."

After the initial leap of faith, and the thrill of being caught, the flyer must now safely swing out with the catcher, perform a 180-degree turn, catch the fly bar, and return to the platform. Although the return may *look* easy, I found it to be deceptively difficult, unglamorous, and definitely not fun! It tormented me like an unrequited love, sucking up countless hours of my time, yet rewarding me with mere scraps of occasional satisfaction. Even if I did successfully beat the odds to make the catch, I could never just relax afterward, breathe a sigh of relief, and bask in the glow of my high-flying achievement. Instead, I had another perilous (yet thankless) trick to perform.

One of my trapeze instructors used to say, "Trapeze is a metaphor for life" —an allegory of how we manage risk, reward, and faith. In my case, the return represented an annoying yet pertinent message about the nature of risk. Some say that risk is its own reward, but I had always believed that my leap of faith would invariably compensate me with something more tangible than a fleeting sense of exhilaration—that following my heart would *instantly bestow* me with financial abundance, a fulfilling relationship, and a life filled with rainbows and butterflies. However, much to my dismay, this wasn't the case.

My leap of faith wasn't enough!

I still had *miles* to go, lessons to learn, and yet another perilous trick to perform!

*She Took the Leap of Faith and
Built Her Wings on the Way Down.*
KOBI AMADA

SECRET SHAME

Unlike guilt, which is the feeling of doing something wrong, shame is the feeling of being something wrong.

MARILYN J. SORENSEN

Bad Debt

So, I admit it. I was wrong! When I agreed to become the CEO of Quantum-Touch, I naively believed that all of the hard work was done. Now I could just sit back, relax, go to the beach, pet the cat, drink a Mai Tai, and wait for the Universe to gift me with loads of prosperity. Surely my courageous leap of faith entitled me to financial abundance, a successful business, and a happy relationship. Right? Do what you love and the money will come. *Isn't that the expression?*

Unfortunately, I allowed the harsh reality of my negative net worth to quickly crush my optimistic belief in a generous, compassionate, and benevolent Universe. I began to lose faith that "the money would come"—because my money was disappearing faster than ice cream on a hot day at the County Fair. Instead of a reliable paycheck, I now had a sporadic stream of income punctuated by no income at all.

On top of that, just nine months after Richard and I moved in together, we ended our romantic relationship. We almost went out of business trying to navigate the challenging emotional terrain of a breakup while continuing to work together. Thankfully, we both recovered from our failed romance relatively quickly and became dear friends. However, our finances were a different story!

In his book *Rich Dad Poor Dad*, author Robert Kiyosaki describes two kinds of debt: "good debt" and "bad debt."

Good debt, such as an investment property, is debt that actually creates wealth, whereas bad debt, such as a car loan, is debt that makes you poor. Given Kiyosaki's emphasis on monetary intelligence, my financial picture would have most likely made him cringe!

During the 2008 economic downturn, we made a heroic attempt to save Quantum-Touch by opening a $100,000 business line of credit. Now, a commercial loan isn't necessarily a bad thing if the money is used to invest in inventory, create new programs, or fund some other profitable venture. However, we used all the money to cover payroll, buy office supplies, pay the electric bill, and basically avoid going out of business—expenses that would never yield a return on our investment. In other words, our entire line of credit qualified as "bad debt!" On top of that, my credit card was maxed out at $35,000 and I had nothing to show for it other than some swanky shoes and a prolific collection of throw pillows—the epitome of bad debt.

In a nutshell, following my heart had generated an un-fathomable amount of bad debt. Worse yet, it caused me to question my integrity as a human being. It contradicted everything I believed in. And it called into question *every-thing* we were teaching others. I felt like a hypocrite. In fact, I *was* a hypocrite by my own standards!

Why couldn't I practice what I preached?

The Force

Well, the Force is what gives a Jedi his power. It's an energy field created by all living things. It surrounds us and penetrates us; it binds the galaxy together.
OBI WAN KENOBI, *STAR WARS*

Allow me to explain the origins of my duplicity. It all started when I attended the Maui Academy of Healing Arts. During the first few weeks of class, I quickly discovered one of the awesome perks of massage school: multiple massages every week! For many students, unlimited bodywork was a small bonus compared to the true payoff of massage school: the opportunity to start a new career. I, on the other hand, knew all along that I had no desire to *actually* work as a massage therapist. So why was I investing an incredible amount of money and time into massage school?

The truth is that I was fascinated by touch. I marveled at the fact that it was so simple yet incredibly powerful. People who are touch-deprived are more likely to feel depressed, stressed, sad, and lonely. On a more positive note, the simple gesture of a loving touch can make an incredible difference in our well-being. (This probably explains why so many people love kittens and puppies.) In my case, just one hug had the capacity to *radically* change my whole outlook for the entire day—and I wanted to know why.

Why was touch so powerful?

I had an intuitive sense that solving this riddle would change my life. And I was right! It forever altered my perception of who we are.

One of the first massage techniques we learned also happened to be my favorite—a light, circular, stroking movement called "effleurage." I loved it because it tended to transport me to a peaceful, meditative state, like a beautiful, flowing dance. I could let my mind go and be totally present with the client.

One day, I experienced something that totally blew my mind. I was in a trancelike state, executing what I believed to be the perfect effleurage, when suddenly the air around my hands became strangely thick and palpable. I sensed a distinct yet subtle pulsation of energy emanating from my client, and I felt an unworldly amount of heat radiating from my hands. I also observed faint traces of light surrounding my hands and the client.

Although I didn't fully understand it at the time, I had just experienced what it's like to "see" and feel "subtle" energy. I had glimpsed the *energy field created by all living beings.* Or, as Obi Wan Kenobi would say, I had just discovered "the Force"!

My experience with the Force taught me that there is more to life than what we can see, hear, touch, or measure. We are more than just our physical body; we are more than a series of chemical reactions; we are more than the product of a mini "super computer" housed in our brain.

We are energetic beings.

And touch is a powerful *exchange of energy.*

My Favorite Magic Trick

Once I discovered the Force, I felt like a zealous kid at Christmastime with a brand-new toy! I became adept at using subtle energy to help people overcome their pain, and I took a gleeful delight in demonstrating the Force around open-minded skeptics. Nothing was more fun than watching their eyes light up in surprise! I loved showing off my favorite "magic trick!"

One Friday night my boyfriend at the time invited me to dinner with friends at a very busy restaurant. When we arrived, we were greeted by a loud and rowdy crowd. I could barely hear anyone at our table over the intense hum of multiple conversations. However, my ears perked up as one of our friends complained about her toothache. She had been hurting for several weeks, felt uncomfortable every time she ate, and was sick of taking aspirin every day. She desperately wanted to be pain-free.

Little did she know, she had just invited me to demonstrate my favorite magic trick. I asked her, "Would you be open to some energy healing?" She was receptive, yet I could tell she wasn't quite sure it would help. Furthermore, the brightly lit, noisy restaurant setting wasn't the most conducive environment for healing. Instead of soft music, candles, and crystals, we were surrounded by chaos and pre-weekend drunken antics. Despite the pandemonium around us, I closed my eyes, focused on her tooth, and sent her energy.

About ten minutes later, her eyes lit up in wonder. Her toothache was gone, and she was pain-free for the first time in weeks! She was very grateful—and surprised!

What exactly did I do?

How could "sending someone energy" actually relieve their pain?

Everything Is Energy

If you want to find the secrets of the universe, think in terms of energy, frequency, and vibration.
NIKOLA TESLA

Taking aspirin to combat pain makes a lot of sense, right? Aspirin prevents the production of pain messengers called prostaglandins, which explains why so many people find it extremely effective. In contrast, "sending someone energy" to relieve pain seems a bit sketchy and hard to believe. How can something so intangible influence the "real world"?

After many years of working with subtle energy, I've come to believe that *everything is energy.* I totally understand how weird and unrealistic this may sound. Everything *seems* so solid. Am I suggesting, for example, that a house isn't as real as it seems? That the wood siding, plastic pipes, metal sink, stainless steel refrigerator, and hardwood floor are all just *energy*? What about the human body? Am I implying that the solidity of our legs, arms, and ears is merely an illusion?

Yes, this is exactly what I'm suggesting!

My belief about the nature of reality is actually backed

up by science. Quantum theory is a branch of physics that explains the nature of matter and energy on the atomic and subatomic level. (We're talking about particles that are a million times smaller than a strand of human hair!)

Although the world around us *appears* to be made up of solid objects—a desk, a chair, a lamp—according to quantum theory, what we perceive as our physical world is really not physical or material at all. In fact, multiple Noble Prize-winning physicists have proven time and time again that *matter is an illusion* and everything in the Universe is actually *made out of energy*.

One reason scientists believe this is due to the principle of superposition. Now, don't worry, I'm not going to dive headfirst into a monotonous, long-winded discussion. A brief overview is all we need.

Let's begin by describing the behavior of particles on the quantum scale. Atomic and subatomic particles can exist in different states. For example, they can be in different positions, have different energies, or be moving at different speeds. Now, here's the strange part about the quantum universe: instead of being in only one state or changing between a variety of states (as we would expect in the real world), a particle acts like a probability wave, *existing across all the possible states at the same time.* This peculiar situation is known as a quantum superposition. Ultimately it suggests that particles are capable of being in an infinite number of states simultaneously, which, according to physicists, *is only possible if everything is energy at the most fundamental level.*

Quantum superposition is rather hard to comprehend, especially if we attempt to apply it to everyday objects. For example, imagine we have a pet kitten named Schrödinger. Like most rambunctious kittens, Schrödinger harbors the uncanny ability to quickly transform any well-decorated living room into a disheveled mess. Apparently, he's a kitten of many talents, extremely proficient at chewing holes in throw pillows, scratching the couch until it's threadbare, puking on the rug, and voraciously eating "nonfood" items.

Now, in the world as we know it, it's *impossible* for Schrödinger to climb the curtains *and* scratch the couch *and* sit on our lap, all at exactly the same time. However, in the strange and counterintuitive state of quantum superposition, Schrödinger would exhibit all of these kitten behaviors (and more) *simultaneously*. In other words, if Schrödinger were a quantum particle, he would be snuggling on our lap, shredding a roll of toilet paper, using the litter box, and doing everything else a kitten could possibly do—*all at the same time.*

And here's something that's even *more bizarre* about quantum superposition: Schrödinger will continue to do everything simultaneously *until we observe him.* (I'll explain this oddity in a minute.)

Admittedly, all of this makes *no sense* to our linear and logical mind. Even Richard Feynman, a theoretical physicist who won the Nobel Prize, acknowledged how peculiar the quantum world is when he said: "I think I can safely say that nobody understands quantum mechanics!" However, despite the bizarre reality of the quantum world, many physicists (and spiritual gurus) agree that the materialistic commonsense notion of reality is actually an *illusion*. In this light, Richard Conn Henry, professor of Physics and Astronomy at Johns Hopkins University, proffered a concise and curt message to the critics of quantum theory: "Get over it and accept the inarguable conclusion. The universe is immaterial-mental and spiritual."

The Copenhagen Interpretation

Clearly the quantum reality appears to drastically conflict with the way we perceive the world. Personally, I've never seen objects exist in multiple states at the same time, have you? That would be weird, right? In the "real world," for example, it's impossible for Schrödinger to nap on the couch and pee in the plant at the same time. Yet in the quantum world, he's doing all of this and more simultaneously!

How then do we explain this discrepancy?

Well, this question is a source of debate among scientists and philosophers. Although scholars have developed multiple theories to describe the relationship between quantum physics and the "real world," the most commonly taught explanation is known as the Copenhagen Interpretation.

In short, the Copenhagen Interpretation implies that the world as we know it can only take place if some sort of measurement or observation occurs. In other words, a particle exists in all possible states at once—until we observe it. Once we observe its state, the superposition collapses and we now have a particle in one known state.

Let's apply the Copenhagen Interpretation our beloved kitten, Schrödinger. In a state of quantum superposition, Schrödinger is doing everything a kitten possibly could, all at one time. Essentially, in a state of superposition, he's not a "real" kitten as we know it. Instead we could think of him as a wave of energetic possibilities, hovering in a ghostly state between existence and nonexistence. However, once we observe him, we collapse the wave of superposition, and our kitten now appears to be doing just one thing, such as licking his tail or destroying our favorite pillow.

In essence, the Copenhagen Interpretation suggests that our reality responds to *consciousness* itself. The world as we experience it is the result of human consciousness interfacing with the quantum levels of existence.

The Law of Attraction

All of this brings up another question. What *exactly* does it mean to "observe" something?

Apparently, this is yet another topic of debate in physics, philosophy, and even computer science. This conundrum is called the "mind-body" problem, and it poses the question, "What is the meeting point between mind and matter?"

As we mentioned before, there is a field of energy (the Force) that emanates from all living things. Everyone seems to have a different "flavor" or *frequency* of energy. In a similar way, every apple has a subtly unique taste. This "field of energy" is also commonly referred to as someone's *vibration*. And many scientists and spiritual gurus suggest that *it's our vibration* that causes a *specific reality* to manifest from the superposition of all possibilities. In other words, when we "observe" something, we are actually *projecting our vibration* onto what we are observing. As one of my favorite comedians, Jim Carrey, suggests:

"Our eyes are not viewers, they're also projectors."

Furthermore, we manifest a *particular reality* through a process that is commonly referred to as the *Law of Attraction*. This law describes a fundamental property of the Universe: *like attracts like*. In other words, there is an attractive, magnetic power of the Universe that draws similar energies together.

For example, if we're feeling depressed, we'll tend to attract people into our lives who are also feeling discouraged and bummed out. If we're angry, we'll attract more things to be angry about, such as a baby that won't stop crying on a long, overnight flight, or an empty roll of toilet paper at an inopportune moment. If we're feeling shy, our beloved Schrödinger will also exhibit this trait and try to hide under the couch when guests arrive. Our money is not immune to the Law of Attraction either. According to the late entrepreneur Jim Rohn, our income is the same as the average income of our five closest friends. (We'll talk about how to shift our vibration around money in much more detail later on.)

So, here's the bottom line: according to the Law of Attraction, our vibration creates the world around us. In other words, we attract what we are in vibrational resonance with. The energy we project is the energy we receive. One of my all-time favorite quotes sums this up quite well:

> *Everything is energy, and that's all there is to it. Match the frequency of the reality you want, and you cannot help but get that reality. It can be no other way. This is not philosophy. This is physics.*

By the way, this quote is often misattributed to Einstein—which is not surprising since it seems like *everything* (except perhaps the Declaration of Independence) has been attributed to him at some point! However, the actual author is Bashar, a multidimensional being who speaks through channel Darryl Anka.

Energy Healing

The physicists are coming to the same conclusion that the mystics had—that it is just the VIBRATION from which everything came into being.
DR. BASKARAN PILLAI

Now, back to my friend with a toothache. According to the Law of Attraction, my friend's toothache was a *reflection of her vibration*. In other words, she attracted her toothache. So, by working with her energy, I was able to help my friend shift her vibration, which caused her tooth-ache to go away.

Let me describe what I did to help her "shift her energy."

When I first started to work on my friend, I closed my eyes, tuned out the chaotic restaurant, and made a conscious choice to "connect with her energy." In other words, I opened up my perception so I could feel, "see," and observe her unique energy field (or vibration.) For a long time, I had to touch someone to feel their energy, yet as I continued to work with subtle energy, I discovered how to feel someone's energy without touching them. (The ability to work with energy at a distance comes in handy in settings like that busy restaurant, where "laying on of hands" might look a bit strange.)

After I connected to my friend's energy, I used a few of my favorite energy healing techniques, including Quantum-Touch to encourage her to *shift her vibration*. I visualized her tooth as whole, complete, balanced, and harmonious, and I imagined that her healing *was already complete*. Superimposing a harmonious vibration with her vibration helped *her* create a new, pain-free reality from the realm of all possibilities. And this is how, in the midst of a noisy restaurant on a Friday night, my friend emerged from this healing experience in a state of pain-free wonder. And make no mistake, *she* did all of the work. I simply invited her (energetically) to choose a new reality from the realm of possibilities, and she accepted my invitation.

After many years of being in the energy healing business,

I'm convinced that the best way we can help others is to simply see them as already *whole and complete* from a space of *gratitude and love.* When we see the highest good in others, we help them change their vibration for the better. Our compassionate "observation" actually influences others to create a happier, healthier reality. That's why I love using the Force to help others, even at a distance, amidst the chaos at a lively restaurant!

My Secret Shame

One day, one of my closest friends remarked, "Wow, you exemplify abundance. I hope someday I can be like you." When she said this, I secretly cringed inside because I felt like a hypocrite. True, I had an amazing lifestyle. I owned a beautiful home in Hawaii, worked out with a gorgeous personal trainer, and had closet full of sparkly stilettos. *What more could I want?* To the outside world, it *seemed* like I had an incredible amount of financial freedom! However, what my friend didn't know is that I fueled my "abundant" lifestyle through massive amounts of debt. I appeared to be abundant, yet it was just an illusion. In reality, I was actually *spiritual and broke.*

Do what you love and the money will come.

Right?

Ahem . . . not really.

When it came to money, I was preaching one thing and doing another. My whole business is based on the philosophy that *we can change our reality by shifting our vibration.* Hence, I was riding the enthusiastic bandwagon of "we create our reality" but failing to actually create abundance. Instead, I *blamed* the Universe for my debt. I believed that the Universe "owed" me countless rewards for having the courage to follow my heart and help others. After all, I reasoned, I took a great risk and I deserved a mighty reward. Then, when "the money didn't come, I went into debt to compensate for the apparent shortcomings of this so-called benevolent Universe. Overall, I felt like a martyr for the cause and a fool for "trusting the Universe."

In *theory*, I knew I had the power to change my energy around money, yet I was frustrated because I couldn't use the Force to dig myself out of debt. I found it incredibly ironic that I could effectively help others change their vibration, yet I was incredibly *ineffective* at changing my own! I was teaching people how to create balance in their physical body, yet I couldn't balance my own budget. I talked about the power of love, but behind closed doors, *I was angry at God.* My debt made me a sham, a walking contradiction, the epitome of inauthenticity. In essence, I felt like a health advocate who eats salad during the day and secretly binges on ice cream at night.

My debt was my secret shame.

And eventually all secrets come to light . . .

There are two kinds of secrets. The ones we keep from others and the ones we keep from ourselves.

FRANK WARREN

POLICE CAR EPIPHANY

Being a victim is more palatable than having to recognize the intrinsic contradictions of one's own governing philosophy.

TOM CLANCY

Why Me?

September 2, 2010

At 3:00 a.m. on a crisp fall night in Venice, California, an intruder had, without my knowledge, crawled through an open window in my kitchen. Sadly, my house was incredibly easy to break into because it had *never* occurred to me to lock the windows at night. In fact, sometimes I even forgot to lock the front door, operating under the naïve assumption that God would always protect me, *no matter what*. However, after that ungodly night, this presumption went right out the window (no pun intended), and I started to follow the pragmatic philosophy expressed in the well-known Arab proverb: "Trust in God but tie up your camel."

As I later discovered, the nefarious intruder had turned my house into a shambles, rummaging through all my cabinets and closets, evidently looking to steal money and other valuables. At that time, given that I was spiritual and broke, I didn't have heaps of money, state-of-the-art electronics, heirloom jewelry, or any other expensive artifacts worth stealing. However, the intruder successfully managed to pilfer the only real assets I *did* possess—my wallet and cell phone. And then, apparently unsatisfied with this paltry booty, he decided to make his way into my bedroom, rudely jolting me awake from a deep sleep.

At approximately 3:30 a.m., I opened my eyes to discover *my worst nightmare ever*. A complete stranger was standing at the foot of my bed, awkwardly holding my bathroom towel over his mouth as an ineffective attempt to conceal his face. With his other hand, he was shining a flashlight into my eyes, casting a dim light into the pitch-black bedroom. I was absolutely terrified!

Was this really happening?

Or was it just a bad dream?

I instinctively screamed in terror. My frenzied cries broke the quiet of the predawn early morning hours, prompting the criminal to panic as well. Afraid that I would wake the nearby neighbors, he pulled out a pair of *my* scissors as his weapon of choice and yelled, "Shut the *%&$#?@!* up or I'll cut you into pieces." Apparently, this was one of the most ill-planned robberies ever executed because he hadn't even bothered to bring his own knife!

At that moment, I honestly believed that this man was going to kill me. He seemed mentally unstable, as though one false move could set him off on a destructive and lethal tailspin. Fearing for my safety, I forced myself to stop screaming and tried to back away from the intruder, yet I had nowhere to go in my tiny bedroom. I felt trapped and helpless.

Now what?

I appealed to a higher power, urgently begging God to *please, please, please* get this man out of my house as quickly as possible!

Where *was* God in all of this, anyway?

What kind of God allows his children to run amuck with apparently *no adult supervision whatsoever?*

I'll spare you the gory details of exactly what happened next. However, what I will say is that my awful wake-up call turned into a robbery *and* a sexual assault. Thankfully, the criminal finally left my house at about 4:00 a.m. Although I felt grateful that he was gone, my relief was very short-lived. Sheer terror soon returned. I felt frozen, paralyzed by my own fear, too afraid to move or even get dressed.

What if the intruder returned?

What if someone else broke in?

I debated whether or not to call for help. Surely, I reasoned, law enforcement had better things to do. After all, I had managed to survive the crime without any physical injuries. Furthermore, I felt ashamed and embarrassed; I had succumbed to the sexual whims of a complete stranger, fearing that my life was in danger. I didn't want to admit *that* to anyone! Why not just go back to bed, pretend nothing had happened, and put this horrible night behind me?

The problem was, I *couldn't* go back to sleep! I was petrified to be alone in my own home. I felt horribly vulnerable, isolated, and incapable of protecting myself. So, despite my reservations, I dialed 911. Soon, detectives and police officers filled the house, asking awkward questions and looking for evidence. Honestly, I didn't care at all about the investigation. All I really wanted was to feel safe. And since I apparently could no longer rely on God to protect me, entertaining a house full of armed officers seemed like the next best thing.

As part of the investigation, law enforcement was required to transport me to the Rape Trauma Center (RTC). I felt mortified—the last thing I needed was an invasive exam to help detectives collect further "evidence." How demeaning! Nevertheless, I was too scared and exhausted to object. So, at approximately 6:00 a.m., two police officers escorted me to their car parked in the alley. One of the officers opened the rear car door, and I submissively climbed into the back seat.

The sun was just peeking out over the eastern horizon, and I reflected upon how the innocence of a new day seemed so ironic, considering that I was sitting in the exact same place usually reserved for criminals! Even the seat felt offensive. It had no padding because, as one of the officers explained, it was easier to clean. *Yuck!* I craved the comfort of a hug or a kind word, not what I got—a shameful ride on a hard, plastic seat behind a steel mesh cage.

How the heck did I end up here?

As I watched the sunrise illuminate my darkest moment, I struggled to digest my unthinkable and hellish night. In a short span of a few hours, my life had imploded into a million pieces. I used to believe that humanity was basically good—that people were, in general, loving, compassionate beings. I used to have faith that God was looking out for me. Now my faith had been shattered. I no longer felt safe in the world. Instead of a mission to live my purpose, my life had morphed into a quest for survival. I didn't understand why a *loving God* would allow this to happen—especially to someone who was trying to make a difference in the world. I felt heartbroken and thoroughly betrayed.

While sitting in the back of the police car, my terror had transformed into numbness, as if the sheer intensity of my emotions had overwhelmed my body and spirit and my only recourse was to shut down. I felt dissociated from life, as though I were floating above the scene, somewhere outside of my body. *What if I could simply disappear?* Maybe I could quietly slip away, like an early morning fog that evaporates in the morning sun. Why not just end it all? What was left for me here, anyway?

Out of pure self-preservation, I started to contemplate the practical implications of the crime. I knew I could never live in my house again, yet I didn't know where else to go. My wallet and cell phone were gone, which was another nightmare in itself. I now needed to cancel my credit cards, order another driver's license, get a new phone, attempt to withdraw money with no identification, and complete a bunch of other inconvenient errands that I had no desire to do. In the meantime, how would I be able to drive without a license? Did I still even have my car keys?

And that's when I had an "Aha!" moment that changed me forever.

A Moment of Brutal Honesty

There I was, sitting in the back of a police car—the worst place I could ever imagine. Feeling totally lost, I was completely absorbed in my own world, wondering how the heck I would ever put my life back together.

Suddenly, my ears perked up and my mind chatter came to an abrupt halt. Time ceased to exist. I intuitively sensed that *the God I had just denounced* was earnestly urging me to pay attention.

And then it happened . . . the moment I'll never forget.

Over the police radio, one of officers announced: "We are now transporting the victim to the RTC." Upon hearing the word *victim*, I was taken aback! It disturbed me *immensely*. I couldn't believe that I was being labeled as a "victim"! I felt humiliated and ashamed! I wanted to scream: "No, no, no! You don't know me at all! I'm a powerful leader and entrepreneur! I teach energy healing! I'm a spiritual person! I am certainly *not* a victim! *How dare you?*"

And then it dawned on me . . .

In a moment of brutal self-honestly, I realized that, I *was* living my life like a victim! I constantly blamed something *outside of myself* for the majority of my problems. I worried about money and blamed "the Universe" for my financial despair. I always fell in love with men who just weren't that "into me" and then would blame them. (And I would sometimes blame the Universe for creating unavailable men in the first place!) I lamented about noisy neighbors and barking dogs and then blamed my neighbors for "forcing" me to move! In fact, I wasn't even aware of how much the victim mindset permeated my life. Like the background hum of the highway in Los Angeles, I routinely tuned it out, the result of having lived there for a *very long time.*

Why was I playing the victim when I knew better?

Fueled by my shame and anguish, I made a powerful, heartfelt promise to myself:

I will never be a victim ever again!

It's Not My Fault, Right?

So, did I keep my promise? Well, not exactly . . . The author of *Gulliver's Travels*, Jonathan Swift, once joked, "Promises and pie crusts are made to be broken." And this is exactly what happened to my promise to "never be a victim ever again!" It lasted just about as long as my typical New Year's resolution to give up sugar—which normally ends around 4:00 p.m. January 1st when my love for chocolate overrules any desire to improve my health.

Now, let's be clear. I didn't break my promise because I actually *enjoyed* being a victim. My life of no money, unavailable men, and noisy neighbors wasn't exactly all that much fun. The real issue was that, on some fundamental level, a part of me *believed* that I was a victim. I was honestly under the impression that sometimes life just throws us a random curveball and we simply have to deal with it. Aren't we all victims on some level just by the nature of existing on planet earth?

Some things are simply random acts of evil, right?

After my sexual assault, I spent *years* wrestling with this question. It refused to leave me alone, haunting me like an annoying mosquito that couldn't get enough blood.

In fact, this very question came up immediately after I returned from the Rape Trauma Center. As I stepped out of the police car, I noticed my landlord surveying the front yard, questioning the chaotic crime scene at her rental. The cute white picket fence was now decorated with copious amounts yellow tape stating: "Police line—do not cross." A hoard of curious neighbors surrounded the property, gossiping about the nature of the crime. Inside, the whole house was a horrible mess, thanks to the grubby combination of fingerprint powder, detectives, police dogs, and the intruder. After assessing damage, my landlord looked at me and coldly remarked, "What kind of trouble did you get yourself into now?" I was appalled! Did she have no empathy? How could she say such a thing?

This crime scene certainly wasn't *my* fault! Right?

Searching for the sympathy my landlord failed to provide, I called a spiritual healer and long-time friend. I rambled on and on about my horrific crime. Expecting some soothing words, I was absolutely taken aback by his response:

"Why would you create that?"

What?

I couldn't believe it! Where did a gal need to go to find some compassion? I felt extremely offended and hurt. Needless to say, that phone call didn't last very long. How dare he blame me when I was clearly suffering and in need of empathy. After all, I had just been the *victim* of a horrendous crime!

But was I really?

On one hand, I had to admit that my spiritual healer (and perhaps even my landlord) made a good point. My entire business is built on the Law of Attraction—the premise that we create our reality. So, I was horrified when the police identified me as a "victim" because it contradicted everything I was teaching others. We surely can't create our reality if we adopt the passive, disempowered stance of a victim.

On the other hand, I was ashamed to admit that I questioned the very philosophy on which my business was built. I found it difficult to believe that the Law of Attraction actually applied to absolutely *everything* in my life. Although I outwardly claimed that I was the powerful architect of my reality, underneath it all I felt like the unwitting victim of a Universe that didn't love me.

Good grief! I was a walking contradiction. I just couldn't reconcile my two opposing points of view:

Am I a really a victim?

or

Do I create everything in my reality?

I questioned whether or not the Law of Attraction truly applied to my robbery and sexual assault. I couldn't have possibly attracted *that*, right? Surely it must have been just a "random act of evil." In this case, I was merely a victim of an arbitrary and horribly cruel world. I was more than happy to congratulate myself for creating all of the good things in my life. Yet when faced with something disturbing and dreadful, I had all kinds of resistance to the idea that I created it!

Why would I manifest my own worst nightmare?

I also had a really tough time believing that the Law of Attraction had any bearing on my finances. I considered myself a responsible and intelligent person, impeccable with my word. So it was difficult for me to believe that I *created* such a huge amount of debt, no savings, and constant stress about money! I honestly thought that my money issues were out of my control—again, like some random act of evil.

Every day we hear stories about the loving mom who is heartbroken over the death of her child, the abuse of an innocent animal, or a virtuous family that loses their home in a flood. How could I possibly accept that nice, decent people *attract* all of these heart-wrenching, insane, and dramatic challenges?

Isn't it rather audacious, insulting even, to imply that we *create* such atrocities?

Aren't certain circumstances simply beyond our control?

THE LAW OF ATTRACTION REVISITED

*The Universe is conspiring to give you
everything you want.*

ABRAHAM HICKS

*Really? No offense, Abraham-Hicks,
but that's hard to believe . . .*

JENNIFER NOEL TAYLOR

(At least that's what I thought back on September 2, 2010.)

Insomnia

I will not sleep until I find a cure for my insomnia.
author unknown

Why do bad things happen to good people? At some point or another, I'm sure each of us has wrestled with this age-old question. It's certainly hard to understand why a *supposedly* loving God would allow horrible, traumatic, and even fatal tragedies to occur. Surely an all-powerful deity could intercept a mass shooting, stop the horrific murder of a child, reroute a destructive hurricane, or prevent a fatal plane crash. Why doesn't God just wave his and hand and make all of our suffering go away?

Speaking of suffering . . .

The aftermath of my sexual assault seemed even worse than the crime itself. As a result of my horrible night, I developed Post-Traumatic Stress Disorder (PTSD). Like a frightened feral kitten, I felt anxious and jumpy all the time. I had an extremely difficult time coping with the most basic things in life, such as summoning the motivation to work, getting a new driver's license, or standing alone on a street corner, even *during the day.*

By the same token, something as simple as a good night of sleep had become painfully elusive. Before my sexual assault, I enjoyed eight hours of deep, uninterrupted sleep almost every night. After my "wake-up" call from this allegedly loving Universe, I found it incredibly difficult to sleep through the night. Thanks to my PTSD, I had developed a debilitating new nightly routine. First, I would wake up numerous times with my heart pounding, petrified that someone would break in again. Next, I would drag myself out of bed and compulsively check every window. Then I would peer down the street to make sure no one was coming. Sometimes, when I was feeling particularly paranoid, I would check all of my closets to make absolutely sure an intruder wasn't hiding in the house. Night after night after night was a battle between fear and exhaustion. I deeply resented my panic-induced insomnia.

I spent a lot of time angrily begging God for some answers. "Why me?" I demanded. Why didn't God intervene? After all, the Universe is *supposed* to reward "good" people and punish the "bad." Right? I had devoted my life to helping others. So why did it seem like I was being punished? Surely I didn't *deserve* that atrocity. Worse yet, my PTSD was seriously interfering with my ability to run Quantum-Touch and fulfill my life purpose. I didn't understand why a loving God would sabotage my efforts to make the world a better place. As far as I was concerned, my sexual assault should have never happened. It seemed so unfair!

Desperate to find the answers God apparently was refusing to provide, I visited a world-famous spiritual healer. I believed that once I solved the riddle of "why me?" my life would go back to normal. So, in hopeful anticipation that I would soon understand the mysteries of the Universe, I told the celebrity healer about my horrific night. His jaw dropped in shock and surprise, and he proceeded to bundle me up in blankets. He then took a seat across the room in a chair a facing me and started to do his healing work. I closed my eyes and waited, eagerly anticipating some profound healing energy or meaningful words of wisdom. I had faith that I would walk away from the session with peace of mind and the ability to sleep soundly through the night again.

About ten minutes into the session, I slowly opened one eye to observe what he was doing and discovered that he had promptly fallen asleep! I couldn't believe it! His easy slumber seemed to make a mockery of my sleepless nights—the reason I came to see him in the first place. My hopes were dashed. I left the session two hundred dollars poorer and still with no answers.

Needless to say, I didn't sleep very well that night.

A Shamanic Vault

Continuing my quest for answers, I signed up for a series of sessions with another spiritual healer. This one was well known for his ability to connect with spirit guides, ascended masters, angels, and even people who have passed on. At this point, I was incredibly exhausted, discouraged, and depressed. I was willing to do whatever it took to get over my PTSD, even if that meant hundreds upon hundreds of sessions and thousands of dollars! I seriously needed to feel safe in the world again.

I worked with this spiritual healer for over a year, and

although we did countless hours of healing work, there is one session in particular I'll never forget. While we were discussing the sexual assault, he relayed a shocking and perplexing message:

> *"If you were in a bank vault with armored walls and a tightly fashioned door sealed shut with a complex lock, the crime still would have happened."*

What!

How unnerving!

He was implying that not only do we create our reality, but we are so powerful that we are capable of creating an experience that doesn't even make sense—our reality is so fluid that anything is possible. This means that I would have attracted the sexual assault, *no matter where I was or what I was doing*, even if I had a security system, a body guard, and fifty locks on my doors and windows.

Although I really wanted dismiss his message as complete New-Age gibberish, I just couldn't let it go. A part of me resonated with what he was saying, and I couldn't help but wonder:

Perhaps we really do create *everything* in our lives?

It Is Manifested

I have a confession to make . . . My session with the psychic healer wasn't the first time I came face-to-face with the distressing suggestion that I created my own worst nightmare.

On the night of the sexual assault, I received a powerful and haunting message that challenged my belief in "random acts of evil." It was so disconcerting and difficult to digest that I told no one about it. Instead I carefully tucked it away in the back of my mind, managing to block it out of my memory—until that disturbing session with my spiritual healer.

Here's what happened . . .

We all have a "still small voice" inside us that offers us guidance through our most difficult challenges. Doreen Virtue, author of *Angel Visions* (and many other books about angels), recounts numerous stories where people avoided a horrible accident or a dangerous situation because they listened to their inner voice.

In my case, right before I was rudely awakened by the intruder, I received an alarming message from my still small voice. I clearly heard:

"It is manifested."

Upon hearing this directive, I understood exactly what it meant. I *knew* I was going to wake up to a horrific situation with an intruder in my room. Worse yet, my pleas for mercy were deliberately denied. Knowing that the Universe is all powerful, I begged: "Please, God, can't I get out of it?" Much to my horror, the Universe responded with a resounding "No." However, those prophetic words did provide a moment of grace—a tiny ray of awareness that acted as a buffer between me and the atrocity I was about to experience.

One of the most disturbing parts about my awful night was that message from my still small voice. The Universe had made it very clear that my nightmarish ordeal was not a random accident.

It was a deliberate manifestation . . . and I created it.

I Think, Therefore I Am?

Part of my resistance to this whole "we create our reality" idea was due to my complete and utter failure to understand *how* the Law of Attraction actually works. Why would I supposedly manifest my own worst nightmare?

It's commonly taught that the Law of Attraction manifests through our thoughts—that the Universe simply responds to our thoughts, without judging whether we are "good" or "bad." Yet, the idea that my thoughts alone created the crime seriously annoyed me because it just didn't seem to be true!

Case in point: before the sexual assault, I hadn't even *considered* the idea that I would someday wake up to a stranger in my bedroom. I didn't entertain nightmarish fantasies involving intruders, rape, or crime. I always felt safe at night, even when I lived alone, and even in Los Angeles. In fact, as I mentioned before, I used to feel so safe that sometimes I would forget to lock the door. In short, I had absolutely no premonition of the horror to come.

So, if my *thoughts alone* were responsible for creating my reality, then the crime should never had happened!

How could I create a reality I had never even imagined?

Mary Poppins to the Rescue

The next phase of my healing journey began quite by accident. Despite having spent thousands and thousands of dollars on a plethora of different therapies, I still had PTSD, routinely suffered from insomnia, and still didn't understand "why bad things happen to good people." Although I was open to the idea that I attracted the crime, I still didn't understand *why*, so I constantly worried I would attract it again. I felt resigned to the fact that I would never get a good night for the *rest of my life*. It was a deeply disturbing thought.

Then one day I ran into a couple I had briefly worked with almost two decades ago. They always had reminded me of Mary Poppins and her magical bag of tricks because not only did they have a cheery disposition, they also employed a wide range of healing techniques, including tantra, talk therapy, energy healing, bodywork, nonviolent communication, and their own unique methods. Even though I was on the verge of giving up, I *still* felt very drawn to work with them. I convinced myself to go to one of their workshops and, as it turned out, I loved their work so much, I ended up attending multiple workshops and participating in private session work over a span of several years.

When I began my healing work with this multifaceted couple, I still had difficulty feeling safe in the world. To the casual observer, I might have appeared functional, maybe even happy. Yet on the inside I constantly felt jumpy and on high alert for danger. Not only had I lost my ability to trust people, I didn't trust God anymore either. Out of pure self-preservation I had fabricated some pretty substantial walls around my heart.

After a year or so of consistent session and group work with this couple, I felt a little better about life over-all. However, I was still plagued by PTSD and sleepless nights—it seemed that no matter what I did, I just couldn't get over that horrible night.

Why couldn't I just move on with my life?

I constantly berated the Universe for my miserable existence and pleaded with God to "please, please have mercy and grant me peace of mind." I was seriously at the end of my rope. Well, either God took pity on me or perhaps I was ready to understand "why me" because my prayers were finally about to be answered.

Linchpin

linch·pin (noun): a central cohesive source of support and stability
"When the linchpin is removed, the walls will crumble."
PRINCETON UNIVERSITY LEXICAL DATABASE FOR ENGLISH

Any emotion we don't fully experience and process can get trapped in the body. This happens because it's natural to repress our feelings when they seem overwhelming or even inappropriate. For example, while I was sitting in the back of the police car, my intense feelings of terror were so overwhelming that they eventually turned into emotional numbness.

Constantly repressing our feelings has a significant downside. Although we may no longer *feel* emotionally triggered, our unprocessed feelings don't just go away. Instead they get buried deep inside, where they can wreak havoc with our health, relationships, finances, or other aspects of our lives. These stuck emotions often rise to the surface during healing work. In fact, that's the whole point! We seek out healing work because we *want* to release the stuck emotional energy that interferes with our general joy for life.

Having already done a *lot* of session work, I was under the naïve impression that I had already processed the majority of my emotional "stuff." So, you can imagine my surprise, when one day, right in the middle of a private session, we unearthed an intense rage and heartbreak that had been stuck deep within the recesses of my heart. My anger felt like a powerful hurricane, capable of destroying everything in its path. Shocked by the depth of my rage, I dissolved into tears. It felt like we had dislodged giant linchpin and the walls around my heart had crumbled into a million pieces.

What was I so angry about?

Up until that point, my dating life could be summed up in two incredibly painful words: unrequited love! It seemed like every man that I ever loved had abandoned me. Some even left without even saying good-bye! In addition, the sexual assault was *not* the first time I had felt violated by a man. To make matters worse, I tended to bury these negative feelings because I believed that "nice" people should never get angry. Moreover, I felt genuinely conflicted about my own anger. On one hand, I loved men. I was attracted to them. I loved feeling safe in the arms of the man that I loved. On the other hand, most of the men in my life had been a source of heartbreak, violation, and betrayal.

After that session, I allowed myself to feel the full intensity of my rage for several days, completely diving into it without judgment or suppression. Even though I was shocked by the ferocity of my feelings, I decided not to shy away from them. Instead I surrounded my anger with love. Much to my amazement, my vile, all-consuming, soul-wrenching rage started to dissipate. In fact, over a period of several days, my anger gradually felt lighter and lighter, and eventually it disappeared altogether! As the old saying goes, "Love is the ultimate healer." In essence, my love acted like a powerful universal solvent for my equally potent negative emotions.

In the midst of processing my anger, the still small voice gently explained that *my intense rage had manifested the crime*. In other words, my anger was the *frequency of energy* that attracted the crime, even though it was buried it deep within my heart. The break-in wasn't the result of my thoughts; it wasn't due to my bad karma, and it wasn't because I was a bad person. I didn't "deserve" to be violated;

no one deserves to be raped or assaulted. The Universe was merely responding to my vibration. Even though I was not fully aware of it, my intense anger was emitting a powerful energy that attracted an equally powerful and horrible experience. The crime just brought my anger to the surface for me to see.

In the Bible, the Greek word for *forgiveness* literally means "to let go." I never fully understood what this meant until I processed the intensity of my rage. Although many people believe that forgiveness is about absolving someone for their "bad" behavior, I realized that my act of forgiveness wasn't about the criminal at all.

It was about me.

After I let go of my resentment, anger, and grief, I felt better than ever. I was liberated from the heavy emotional baggage that I had been lugging around—a lifetime of enmity, sadness, and bitterness. On some strange level, I emerged from my healing quest with a sense of gratitude for the crime; it had created an opportunity for me to heal my heart.

Let me clarify something: forgiveness is *not* about *excusing* the behavior of someone else. It's never acceptable to abandon, steal, threaten, rape, or harm someone else. Instead, letting go benefits us. It changes our frequency, which inevitably changes what we attract into our lives. In other words:

Forgiveness releases the frequency of energy that is responsible for manifesting a particular reality.

As one of my favorite authors, Doreen Virtue, wrote, "Forgiveness doesn't mean that what they did is okay. . . . It means that you are no longer willing to carry toxic anger in your heart." In my case, not only did my PTSD go away, my *entire* life changed for the better. After releasing the anger in my heart, I no longer attracted men who violated my boundaries or treated me with disrespect.

Overall, discovering my "linchpin" was extremely disquieting and exciting at the same time. I was disturbed to find out that my heart could hold on to so much anger, especially given the fact that I did spiritual healing for a living. And yet I was excited to emerge from my emotional process with a new understanding of the Law of Attraction. As my psychic healer suggested, I would have attracted the sexual assault in a tightly sealed bank vault. There are no "random acts of evil." We do attract every experience in our lives. The law of attraction is a *universal law.*

We create our reality—*no exceptions.*

We are *always* a perfect "vibrational match" for the circumstances in our life. This is not merely philosophy. *It is physics.*

And who wants to argue with Mother Nature?

The Heart Wants What It Wants

The heart wants what it wants.
It doesn't seek other people's opinions;
sometimes not even your own.
STEVE MARABOLI

So now I knew. I manifested my own nightmare. My unprocessed rage and lack of forgiveness created that traumatic night. My heart had been trying to tell me something, and apparently it took a huge wake-up call (literally!) for me to get the message. On my quest to understand "why me?" I discovered how powerful my heart really is.

The heart is so dynamic because it represents the energy and essence of who we are, *our vibration as multidimensional beings*. As the French philosopher and Jesuit priest Pierre Teilhard de Chardin said, "We are spiritual beings having a human experience." We are much more than just our bodies, our thoughts, or even our minds. There is a part of us that is eternal, that exists beyond time and space, which is our spirit. And then there is a part of us that is human, mortal, flesh and blood, which is our body. Our heart is the bridge between both of these aspects of ourselves. It's the link between spirit and body.

Now, I believe that we came to earth to do much more than just enjoy the beautiful scenery, hugs, kittens, and chocolate . . .

First of all, we are here to serve others by living our

purpose. Everyone has a specific mission; there are no accidents or meaningless lives. My purpose is energy healing. Yours may be writing a book, designing a new computer, teaching children, developing electric vehicles, or comforting the homeless. We are here to help others in a meaningful way. And our heart acts like a compass that is always guiding us toward our true calling, urging us to do what we came here to do. This is why I was compelled to quit my job and pursue energy medicine. My heart was telling me to live my purpose, and I felt destined to take a leap of faith, even if it was scary or seemingly crazy! Our heart attracts certain experiences to constantly nudge us toward our true calling in life.

Second, I believe we are here to grow spiritually. We are here to learn how to love and be loved. The Universe is constantly urging us to open our hearts more fully and love more deeply. If our heart has any walls around it, such as limiting beliefs, stuck emotions, anger, or negative thoughts, we will attract experiences to help us see the truth within. In my case, I attracted the sexual assault because of unprocessed rage in my heart; carrying around all that anger prevented me from fully opening my heart. Although the crime was the worst night of my life, something good came from it—I evolved. As the Bible says, "In all things God works for the good of those who love him." As I see it, from great tragedy we can emerge, not with a broken heart, but with our heart *broken open*.

Our heart is the attractive, magnetic power of the

Universe that draws similar energies together. The Universe is not just some sort of cosmic Santa Claus that rewards the "good" people and punishes the "bad." Instead, as Dr. Wayne Dyer said, "We attract what we are." Our heart attracts our experiences, nudging us to love more deeply, evolve spiritually, and live our purpose.

At long last, I understood the answer to "why me?"

Now I could finally get some sleep.

You have to keep breaking your heart until it opens.
RUMI

SELECTIVE OWNERSHIP

*Responsibility: No single drop of water thinks
it is responsible for the flood.*

AUTHOR UNKNOWN

Vertigo

The key to keeping your balance is knowing when you've lost it.
AUTHOR UNKNOWN

Feeling deeply disheartened, I sat yet again in another doctor's office. I was absolutely miserable. Even though I was just a senior in high school, I felt like I had more health problems than an obese eighty-year-old alcoholic with advanced liver disease! Thanks to severe allergies, I spent the majority of my childhood reluctantly patronizing a wide assortment of various medical establishments. This time, my mom had dragged me to an ear, nose, and throat (ENT) specialist, who, after careful examination, stated: "Your ears are not draining properly." When I heard his seemingly useless diagnosis, I wanted to scream! I already knew that my ears were clogged up. In fact, they were so congested, I could barely hear anything, including the doctor!

It seemed like I was allergic to *everything*. My body was a lean, mean, mucous-producing machine, operating non-stop twenty-four hours a day. Although I didn't have a lot of friends growing up, I did have one faithful companion: a soggy and shredded tissue. I would begin my day stuffing my pockets with what I believed to be an abundance of tissues, certainly enough to last me. Yet by the end of the day, my supply would always run dangerously low, forcing me to preserve my last remaining tissue at all costs, no matter how gross it became. Since I couldn't breathe through my nose, I became a habitual mouth-breather, resulting in a never-ending chronic case of dry mouth. My sinuses always felt like a waterlogged, worn-out sponge. Between the constant sinus pressure, dry mouth, burning eyes, and overly used tissues, I resented the fact that my allergies were so debilitating. I hated them, and I hated being sick all the time. I just wanted to be a normal kid.

My allergies tended to flare up at the most surprising and inopportune times. For example, during one holiday season, our church proudly displayed a live pine Christmas tree on the festive altar. Elegantly adorned with white lights, angels, and gold ornaments, the tree looked stunning. Although most people were impressed by its beauty, I was astonished by my body's unfortunate and severe reaction to the tree. While churchgoers sang their hymns and prayed in peaceful harmony, I had multiple sneezing fits. Apparently, I had a serious allergy to pine trees!

My parents had tried everything they could to help me. When I was five years old, I underwent an adenoidectomy and tonsillectomy. After that, we tried allergy shots, over-the-counter medications, skin testing, and even a "state of the art" prescription antihistamine called Seldane. However, much to my dismay, no matter how much the doctors poked, prodded, and prescribed, I never found any lasting relief. Sadly, I spent the majority of my childhood feeling betrayed by my own body.

Worse yet, the sinus pressure often led to vertigo, which I found particularly frustrating because it interfered with my lifelong dream to become an Olympic gymnast. When I was six years old, my parents enrolled me in a tumbling class and I immediately fell in love with gymnastics. I spent almost all my time at the gym, working hard to make my dream a reality. Yet, the vertigo often disrupted my workouts, causing me to lose my balance in the middle of my routines and forcing me to take time off from the gym. I blamed my allergies for sabotaging my biggest hopes and dreams.

My vertigo became really bad during my senior year in high school, prompting the visit to the ENT. Although I felt disheartened by this lifelong challenge, I still hadn't given up. I had high hopes that this doctor would work his magic and fix my ears. So, per the doctor's advice, I subjected myself to a myringotomy: a painful ear operation that involves making a tiny incision in the eardrum and then inserting a plastic tube. The tube is supposed to help the eardrum equalize the pressure and keep the middle ear aerated. This procedure seemed like an answer to my prayers. I felt extremely optimistic!

However, after the surgery, the tubes didn't seem to work at all. In fact, I felt worse! I *still* had the vertigo. My ears still felt clogged and now, on top of that, I was in a lot of pain as a result of the surgery. Also, I had be extra careful in the shower because I could risk getting an infection if I got water in my ears. The entire ordeal seemed like a colossal waste of time and energy. Eventually the tubes fell out and I was back to where I started—extremely frustrated by my chronic allergies.

Soon after my regretful myringotomy, I enrolled at Cal Poly (California Polytechnic State University) and moved to San Luis Obispo, California, eager to leave my old life behind and start a new chapter. Yet unfortunately, I couldn't leave the allergies behind. They interfered with my ability to attend classes, do homework, and concentrate during exams. When my vertigo caused me to bump into walls and lose my balance, my classmates teased me about my clumsy tendencies. I pretended to laugh with them, yet underneath it all, I felt very hurt. Even though I visited the student medical clinic multiple times a week, I still felt fatigued and miserable most of the time. Once again, my allergies were disruptive to my life and dreams.

During my senior year, I finally hit a wall. Maybe I had "senioritis," but I was just sick and tired of being sick and tired. I was tired of getting allergy shots. I was sick of taking Seldane twice a day. And I hated the idea of taking medication for the rest of my life. Not only was it expensive, it didn't seem that effective anyway. Something needed to give.

Speaking of hitting a wall, in a pamphlet published in 1981, the twelve-step program Narcotics Anonymous defined insanity as "repeating the same mistakes and expecting *different* results." (Incidentally, this is *another* quote often misattributed to Einstein.) Apparently, I was insane because I had spent *years* battling my soul-sucking allergic rhinitis with the same ineffective treatments over and over again.

I was weary from the fight.

So, I did something I wholeheartedly *do not* recommend

for anyone else. Out of sheer desperation, I quit going to the doctor "cold turkey." I threw my medication away, stopped going to the Cal Poly medical clinic, and vowed to never visit another doctor ever again. Even though I wasn't sure of my next step, I decided to eliminate what obviously was not working. It was time to take matters into my own hands.

And that is when I finally found my balance.

Nothing to Lose

My doctor told me to avoid unnecessary stress,
so I stopped going to doctors.
AUTHOR UNKNOWN

Once I quit going to the doctor, I felt incredibly relieved. I no longer felt compelled to suffer through another allergy shot or medical examination. Nevertheless, although I had given up on doctors, drugs, and surgery, I still hadn't given up on finding an antidote.

I just needed a new approach.

So, with renewed optimism, I did my own research on ways to overcome allergies *naturally*. I tried acupuncture, massage, and herbs. I experimented with my diet and eliminated dairy and wheat. I stopped drinking diet soda and drank more water instead. Much to my amazement, these changes began to pay off. As I started to feel better, my life-long despair transformed into hope. I sensed that I was on the right path, even though I wasn't fully cured.

After a few years of "taking matters into my own hands,"

I made a shocking discovery that ended my lifelong battle with allergies for good. My epiphany happened in a very unusual way, at the end of a surprising series of synchronicities. I felt guided to follow a path that was way outside of my comfort zone, something I thought I would never do, not in a million years. Yet I felt strangely compelled by a mysterious Force greater than myself.

Here's what happened . . .

One year after I graduated from Cal Poly, I accepted a job as a software developer in San Luis Obispo, California. I rented a beautiful apartment overlooking the harbor in Morro Bay, and I absolutely loved it! I loved the peace and quiet. I loved the view of the ships at night, with the moonlight shining on the water. And I especially loved living alone. I could wander around naked, crank the heat to a balmy eighty degrees, blast my favorite music, or simply enjoy the sound of silence. My apartment was my own personal Shangri-La, the perfect place to "get away from it all" at the end of a long workday.

Given how much I loved my place, I did something that completely took me by surprise. One day, while reading the paper, I browsed the housing classifieds. (To this day, I have no clue why I did this!) What's even odder is that one of the ads caught my eye. In fact, I felt *compelled* to drive out and take a look at this particular rental. Soon after I arrived, however, I realized that the place had a major deal breaker: it came with five roommates! This meant sharing a bathroom for the first time in years, wading through a disgusting refrigerator crammed full of other people's food, and subjecting myself to loud parties and all-night movie marathons. So, I brushed it off, thinking no way would I ever live there!

Yet I couldn't let it go.

Strangely enough, I felt that the Universe was guiding me to take the rental. So, despite my better judgment, I signed a lease at the new place. I really had no clue what I was getting myself into, other than subjecting myself to a crowded, noisy, and chaotic place to live. I felt as though I had finally gone mad, and I immediately regretted my choice.

After I moved in, I became very curious about my landlord; there was just "something" about him. We started hanging out together and frequently talked late into the night about life, the Universe, and everything in between. One day I launched into a long-winded story about my lifelong struggle with allergies, recounting the endless trips to the doctor, the ineffective drugs, and my disappointing surgery. After patiently listening to my tales of woe, he said something I found very difficult to believe. He told me I could actually *eliminate* my allergies once and for all by following a "raw food" diet.

A raw food diet is a diet that consists only of uncooked fruits, vegetables, nuts, and seeds. The diet is vegan, which means no animal products are consumed—no meat, fish, chicken, or dairy. Furthermore, nothing is heated above 105 degrees, so essentially you never cook your food. My landlord had been following this diet for years, and he said it had helped him improve his health tremendously. He strongly urged me to give it a try.

Despite his optimism, I found his dietary advice hard to digest!

I had a hard time believing that something so simple could eliminate my lifelong, excruciating battle with allergies. On one hand, the idea of eating only raw, unprocessed food actually made a lot of sense to me. After all, animals in the wild don't cook their food. Could you imagine tigers in the wild, catching their prey and then having a BBQ? Wouldn't it be weird if dolphins ate ice cream and cookies? The concept of listening to the wisdom of nature seemed very intriguing to me. On the other hand, I felt very apprehensive about trying a diet that completely contradicted everything I had been taught about nutrition. I grew up believing that a healthy diet consists of eating of foods from the "four food groups": meat, dairy, grains, and fruits and vegetables. How could a diet without meat and dairy actually be good for you?

As author Jodi Picoult once said, "The desperate usually succeed because they have nothing to lose." After years of misery, I definitely qualified as *desperate*! So, despite my misgivings, I decided to give raw food a try. Given that I had no experience with "raw food prep," I subsisted on a diet of dates, macadamia nuts, and simple salads. However, much to my surprise, I actually enjoyed the diet more than I thought I would! I didn't miss my beloved "four food groups" at all.

After following the diet for a week or so, I was absolutely floored by the results. Much to my amazement, my allergies had disappeared! My nose was clear for the first time in years, my ears didn't feel clogged up anymore, and I no longer had to stuff my pockets with tissues before leaving the house.

I could hardly believe it!

Upon further research I discovered that the rapid results I experienced weren't that unusual. Many people have reported overcoming migraines, asthma, allergies, and other health issues in a very short period of time after adopting a raw food diet.

Who knew the answer could be so simple?

Occam's Razor

So, was I grateful? Yes . . . and no. On one hand, I loved letting go of my collection of soggy tissues. I loved being able to breathe like a normal person, pet a cat without sneezing, and enjoy freshly cut grass. On the other hand, I felt betrayed by the simplicity of it all. After all, I had studied computer science, physics, calculus, and logic. I prided myself on my intellectual prowess. I was trained to find intricate solutions to sophisticated intellectual puzzles. Yet it seemed like my lifelong exploration of the complexities of medical science provided me with no real understanding of how the body actually works! I felt humbled, like a queen exiled from her palace of well-bred, rational dogma.

The fourteenth-century philosopher William of Ockham developed a principle called Occam's Razor, which suggests that "the simplest answer is most often correct." Hence, while I was happy to see the end of my allergies, I was also disappointed by the limits of my highly complicated and intellectual approach to life. Perhaps Einstein felt the same way when he said that "all physical theories, their mathematical expressions apart, ought to lend themselves to so simple a description that even a child could understand them." Apparently, I had spent my life ignoring the wisdom behind Occam's Razor!

Empowerment

The 1939 American musical fantasy, *The Wizard of Oz,* was widely considered to be one of the greatest films in cinema history. The movie tells the of story of Dorothy and her dog Toto who live on a Kansas farm. When a tornado strikes, she and Toto are swept away to the magical Land of Oz. Despite the enchanting scenery and colorful residents, all Dorothy wants to do is return home. To this end, Glinda the Good Witch of the North advises her to seek out the aid of the Wizard of Oz, who lives in the Emerald City. Eager to meet the Wizard, Dorothy sets off down the Yellow Brick Road. She encounters many hazards along the way, such as harassment from the Wicked Witch of the West, an attack by evil winged monkeys, and an encounter with poisonous poppies. However, she masterfully overcomes every obstacle and finally arrives at the Emerald City.

Spoiler alert! Much to Dorothy's dismay, the Wizard turns out to be a complete sham. Instead of a powerful magician, he's actually a middle-aged man, hiding behind a curtain and speaking through a microphone. Although Dorothy is devastated by the prospect that she many never return home, all hope is not lost. Glinda appears again and informs Dorothy that she *had the ability to go home all along!* All she needs to do is click together her magical ruby slippers and say, "There's no place like home!" And sure enough, Dorothy finds her way back home.

How ironic, right? Dorothy risked life and limb to get help from a great Wizard, only to discover that she *didn't even need the Wizard after all!* In fact, the magical Wizard was merely a figment of the imagination; he didn't really exist!

My own journey to find a cure for my allergies seemed just as ironic. Initially my decision to quit going to the doctor was simply the result of my extreme frustration, despair, and anger. I gleefully threw away my medication, having little regard to the consequences because frankly, I didn't give a damn anymore.

At the time, I thought I was just "giving up." Yet my decision to "take matters into my own hands" was actually a *powerful shift in consciousness.* Rather than waiting for someone to "fix me," *I stopped giving my power away.* I stopped blaming the marginally effective antihistamine for its inability to make me feel better. I no longer felt frustrated by the doctor, the ENT, or the nurse that gave me shots.

I even stopped blaming my body's overly zealous mucous for my constant misery. Ultimately, I stopped feeling like a "victim" and took *responsibility* for my well-being. I took *full ownership* of my own health.

I had become my own Wizard!

As motivational coach Bob Proctor said, "Everything that you want is already yours. It is simply becoming more aware of what you already possess." Just like Dorothy, I realized that I didn't need a complicated walk on the Yellow Brick Road, a pretentious Wizard, or even a doctor to tell me what to do. Instead, my transformation from victim to owner was a *crucial shift in consciousness* that actually turned my health around.

I had the power all along.

Selective Ownership

Speaking of empowerment . . . Once I took ownership for my health, I enjoyed an immense amount of freedom. My fear of pine trees, dust mites, spring, and long-haired cats became a thing of the past. I finally felt like I was in charge of my own health!

Now don't get me wrong, I didn't enjoy perfect health all of the time. Occasionally, I still experienced a runny nose or watery eyes. However, instead of feeling sorry for myself or getting angry, I just cleaned up my diet, took better care of myself, and my allergies would inevitably disappear. I understood that my allergies were a choice—the result of eating too much junk food, skimping on raw fruits and vegetables, a lack of exercise, and an overall failure to take care of myself. Hence, I never went back to the "poor, sick me" mindset. If I didn't feel well, I knew *exactly* how to fix it.

Oddly enough, prior to my police car epiphany, I didn't enjoy this same level of freedom when it came to money! When I took the leap of faith to do what I love, I felt completely powerless over my mounting credit card bills, lack of income, and out of control expenses. I constantly worried about money. Consequently, I blamed a lot of things for my debt, including God, my business partner, the economy, taxes—and did I mention God? Even though I took full responsibility for my health, when it came to my finances, I felt trapped, like a tiny mouse in an unsolvable maze with no exit in sight.

Here's what I'm getting at: my approach to health was dramatically different than my approach to wealth. When it came to my health, I took full responsibility for my well-being, yet, when it came to my finances, I felt like a helpless victim. This same level of incongruency permeated other areas of my life as well. Once in a while, I actually took responsibility for my problems, yet most of the time I felt victimized by the seemingly unpredictable randomness of the Universe. Overall, my life was a recursive battle between victim and owner. I was a walking contradiction, guilty of what I now call "selective ownership."

Selective ownership is an inconsistent approach to life whereby we vacillate back and forth between victim and

*owner, only willing to take responsibility for a few select aspects
of our experience.*

Selective ownership was certainly a perfect description
of my cognitive dissidence; I simultaneously believed in
two contradictory values. On one hand, I was the CEO of
Quantum-Touch, a company deeply rooted in a core philosophy of ownership. Our healing techniques are based on
the assumption that we create our reality, and I knew better
than to wallow around in the mire of my own martyrdom.
On the other hand, I was very selective in my own ability
to "practice what I preached." Do we create our entire reality or not? I couldn't decide. This hypocrisy was my secret
shame.

It also explains why I was spiritual and broke.

Waiting for God

My version of selective ownership was particularly insid-
ious due to my tendency to blame God for my negative net worth. In fact, I believed that I had every right to
blame God. After all, I had gone out on a limb to help others!
God owed me.

So why he wasn't he doing his part?

While I was fervently praying for financial security, I was
also digging myself deeper and deeper into debt. Surely, I
reasoned, the Universe would soon come to my rescue! I
eagerly awaited the day that my money problems would
finally be over. Sadly, that day never came.

Are you familiar with the parable of the drowning man? It sums up my attitude quite well.

The story goes something like this…

The Parable of the Drowning Man (author unknown)

A terrible storm came into a town, and the local officials sent out an emergency warning that the riverbanks would soon overflow and flood the nearby homes. They ordered everyone in town to evacuate immediately.

A faithful Christian man heard the warning and decided to stay, saying to himself, "I will trust God, and if I am in danger, God will send a divine miracle to save me."

His neighbors said to him, "We're leaving, and there is room for you in our car—please come with us!" But the man declined. "I have faith that God will save me."

As the man stood on his porch watching the water rise up the steps, a man in a canoe paddled by and called to him, "Hurry and come into my canoe; the waters are rising quickly!" But the man again said, "No thanks, God will save me."

The floodwaters rose higher, pouring water into his living room and the man had to climb to safety on the second floor. A police motorboat came by and saw him at the window. "We will come up and rescue you!" they shouted. But the man refused, waving them off and saying, "Use your time to save someone else! I have faith that God will save me!"

The flood waters rose higher and higher and the man had to climb up onto the roof.

A helicopter spotted him and dropped a rope ladder. A rescue officer came down the ladder and pleaded with the man, "Grab my hand and I will pull you up!" But the man *still* refused, folding his arms tightly across his body. "No thank you! God will save me!"

Shortly after, the floodwaters swept the man away and he drowned.

When he got to Heaven, the man stood before God and asked, "I put all of my faith in You. Why didn't You come and save me?"

And God said, "Son, I sent you a warning. I sent you a car. I sent you a canoe. I sent you a motorboat. I sent you a helicopter. What more were you looking for?"

Like the drowning man, I was expecting a divine miracle to rescue me. I believed that "waiting for God" was a demonstration of my steadfast and unwavering faith. However, it was really just the *excuse* I used to *avoid* actually dealing with my financial problems! In other words, *I used my faith to rationalize my victim mindset.* I was insisting that the Universe magically balance my checkbook for me, without actually doing anything about it myself. And then, when the Universe didn't "save me," I felt like a martyr. I was "waiting for God" rather than owning responsibility for my finances.

And that was my mistake.

So, if you're tempted like I was to "wait for God," consider this:

God may actually be waiting for you.

*"You've always had the Power my dear,
you just had to learn it for yourself."*
GLINDA THE GOOD WITCH, *THE WIZARD OF OZ*

THE ESSENTIAL SHIFT

Your time as a caterpillar has expired.
Your wings are ready.
JOHN ASSARAF

Strange Jewels

*Those blocks on your life journey can either be
road blocks or building blocks.*
PATTI KING MAJESKI

Have you ever visited the LEGO Store in New York City? In my humble opinion, it's one of the most amazing places to see in the "Big Apple"! Now, I know what you're thinking. New York is home to the Statue of Liberty, the Empire State Building, Broadway, and Wall Street. How could I possibly compare the LEGO Store to these extraordinary and iconic landmarks?

Don't get me wrong, the Empire State Building is definitely awe-inspiring, especially when you're on the eighty-sixth floor with an incredible 360-degree view of the New York skyline. Likewise, the Statue of Liberty is equally amazing; it's the quintessential symbol of freedom. I'm certainly not discounting the remarkable historical significance of these monumental landmarks.

Nevertheless, when I visited the LEGO Store, I instantly fell in love! I discovered what author Elizabeth Gilbert refers to as the "strange jewels" within. In her book *Big Magic*, she asserts that we all harbor strange jewels inside of us; we all possess unique and brilliant creative capacities, aspirations, and secret talents. She encourages us to do *whatever brings us to life*, suggesting that the secret to unearthing our strange jewels is to follow our own fascinations, obsessions, and compulsions.

In my case, the LEGO Store brought me to life, invoking my creative spirit with its mesmerizing display of mind-boggling and elaborate LEGO inventions. The nostalgic LEGO carousel reminded me of my first trip to Disneyland, enchanting me with its colorful blue-and-gold detailing, a gorgeous white swan, and a delightful moving elephant. The LEGO model of the Statue of Liberty, intricately constructed from over two thousand pieces, was an impressive replica of the real thing. Of course, being a huge Disney fan, my favorite LEGO creation was the Magic Castle. This highly detailed four thousand-piece sculpture featured everything I love about Cinderella's Palace, including the iconic clock with roman numerals, a wide arched entrance, and spired towers.

I fell in love with the LEGO Store because of what it represents: an idyllic and magical world where I have the power and freedom to create anything I could ever want or imagine. In my own private LEGO universe, I could build an elaborate pirate ship and sail around the world, eagerly searching for buried treasure. Or I could engineer my own Magic Castle and populate it with fifty of the most adorable kittens ever. I could even construct my own exclusive bank and enjoy an infinite supply of $100 bills. Furthermore, if I inadvertently managed to invent something I didn't like, I could simply dismantle it and build something new. In this magical world, my creativity is only limited by my imagination.

Wouldn't it be wonderful if we had this same all-encompassing creative freedom in *real life*?

We could build our dream house, pay off all our debt, or manifest our perfect romantic partner—simply by finding the right LEGOs and snapping them into place! Wouldn't it be amazing if our world was like a giant box of LEGOs, with infinite potential to create the life of our dreams?

That's exactly my point!

Our world *is* like a giant box of LEGOs, but instead of plastic, these special LEGOs are composed entirely of *energy*. We can use these energetic building blocks to construct our idyllic and magical world *for real*.

We *can* enjoy limitless creative power and freedom in our lives.

However, there's just one catch . . .

If we want to access our own cosmic LEGOs and unlock our infinite creative potential, we need to change the fundamental way that we perceive ourselves and the world around us.

This is what I call the "Essential Shift."

The Essential Shift

"The moment you accept responsibility for everything in your life is the moment you gain the power to change anything in your life."
HAL ELROD

In chapter three, we talked about the physics behind the Law of Attraction, suggesting that when we view something, we are actually *projecting our energy* onto what we are observing, rather than merely watching the world go by. Furthermore, this act of observation (or our energy projection) *causes* a particular reality to manifest from the realm of all possibilities. As I like to say, the way we *view the world is the way the world views us.*

Pretty trippy, right?

If we want to create a significant change in our life, we need to fundamentally transform the way we view the world. In other words, we need a paradigm shift—a complete overhaul of our frame of reference.

To illustrate what I mean, let me tell you a story . . .

Once upon a time there was an unusually adventurous ant named Arthur who unfortunately found himself trapped in a public library. Tired of scavenging for leftover sandwich crumbs and scraps of powdered doughnuts, he was getting quite antsy. (Sorry, I couldn't resist the pun!) Sadly, his daily quest for food often left him empty-handed (or, according to ant anatomy, empty tarsus-ed).

One day, Arthur was feeling particularly down and out. His next meal was nowhere to be found and he felt depressed; he absolutely hated being hungry all the time. Normally he would have ignored his bad mood and forged ahead, continuing his never-ending search for food. Instead, he sighed in exasperation and wondered:

What's the point?

Why do I struggle day in and day out?

Why is life so hard?

Certainly, there must be more to life than this!

Feeling extremely troubled, Arthur took a deep breath and looked around. Although he had spent countless hours scouring the library for food, he had never paid much attention to the large rectangular objects housed in this strangely quiet place. What were they? And more importantly, why did so many people come here day after day just to visit them?

Encouraged by his newfound curiosity, Arthur decided to embark on a vision quest, hoping for a cosmic sign that there was more to life than just mere survival. As he wandered off in search of a suitable location for introspection, he noticed a particularly alluring and colorful quadratic mountain. He paused, feeling strongly guided to climb it. As he diligently ascended to the top, he realized that the face of this rectilinear mountain was constantly changing colors beneath him; at first it was dark pink, then white, then yellow, then light pink, then blue. Furthermore, it seemed like the different colors formed a pattern of some sort, yet he just couldn't figure out what it was. He started to meander around in circles, trying to understand the seemingly inscrutable design beneath him. What if this colorful terrain harbored the answers to life, the Universe, and everything? Could this be his sign? Arthur prayed for enlightenment, beseeching God to help him understand this mysterious Rosetta Stone.

While Arthur was busy begging the Almighty for answers, the sun was starting to fall behind the horizon. Hoping to complete his quest before nightfall, he continued his journey up the mountain. After what seemed like a very long time (in ant years), he triumphantly reached the top. As he congratulated himself on a successful climb, a large creature pointed his way and exclaimed, "Look Mom! *Big Magic!* It's one of my favorite books."

Flabbergasted, Arthur recognized the profound significance of this magical moment. Here he was, standing on top of B*ig Magic*. Yet, due to his small size, he didn't have the capacity to understand where he was. However, the large creature could easily decipher the title of the book.

Arthur bowed in awe, thanking God for answering his prayers. He realized that everything in life, no matter how small or seemingly insignificant, had meaning! It was all just a matter of perspective. Sometimes we simply need a different frame of reference to perceive the magic right in front of us.

Albert Einstein once said, "No problem can be solved from the same level of consciousness that created it." (As far as I know, Einstein actually said this one!) Nothing could have been more accurate when it came to my finances! As long as I "waited for God" to save me from my money problems, I never managed to make a dent in my debt. In fact, the Universe could have been sending me incredible business opportunities, brilliant financial advisors, effective cost-cutting ideas, and numerous other ways to help me fix my negative net, yet I didn't have the proper frame of reference to recognize the solutions right in front of me. As long as I blamed Spirit/the Universe/All That Is for my lack of money, I was like Arthur the ant, unable to grasp the fact that I was on the precipice of *Big Magic!* Like many of us, I was clinging to my identification as a victim and a "martyr for the cause." What I didn't realize back then is that the *victim mindset is the level of consciousness that was keeping me spiritual and broke.*

As victims, we send out a mixed message to the Universe. On one hand, we are saying yes to abundance. On the other hand, we are *also* telling the Universe that we can't create what we want because, from the victim standpoint, we have no power to change anything or create anything different. It's like trying to go sixty miles per hour down the highway with the brakes on. As long as we blame the economy, the government, our spouse, our boss, God, the Universe, our pets, the "system," or anything else for our underwhelming bank account, we might as well be using $100 bills as kitty litter. We are giving our power away to something or someone outside of ourselves. The victim mentality *prevents* us from ever being a *vibrational match* for abundance. It actually *blocks* us from manifesting what we truly want.

As the late Wayne Dyer said, "Abundance is not something we acquire; it is something we tune into." In other words, our finances are a reflection of what is going on inside of us. So, if we want to profoundly transform our bank account balance, *we first need to make a profound shift in our consciousness.* Letting go of the victim mentality is the most important step we can take toward financial alignment. This shift from *victim* to *owner* allows us to approach our finances from a new perspective and a higher level of awareness. In fact, just this decision itself creates a profound shift in our vibration.

It's the Essential Shift.

The Magic of Ownership

Sometimes when things are falling apart,
they are actually falling into place.
ANURAG PRAKASH RAY

Walt Disney once said, "All our dreams come true if we have the courage to pursue them." I love Disney's optimism, yet, for many of us, our dreams are long forgotten, buried beneath mounds of cynicism and obligations. Seriously, how do we find the time to dream when there are bills to pay, rush hour traffic, piles of laundry, and neighbors from hell? How can we "have the courage to pursue our dreams" if we don't even remember what they are?

Here's a secret I discovered about dreams . . .

Although this may be hard to appreciate, I believe that our challenges and hardships are actually opportunities to manifest our true heartfelt dreams and desires. As Abraham-Hicks suggests, "The Universe is conspiring to give us everything we want." Whether we like it or not, sometimes the Universe helps us "manifest everything we want" by giving us what appears to be an annoying obstacle on our path. We can either perceive this unwanted detour as a massive inconvenience and bemoan our unfortunate fate or we can view it as a "course correction" ultimately leading us toward our true heartfelt dreams. To risk sounding like a well-worn cliché, our problems could actually be blessings in disguise.

Now, I totally understand how irritating this sounds!

Heck, sometimes the "blessing in disguise" adage *still* disturbs me! When we're in the midst of dealing with something heart-wrenching and terrible (such as a sexual assault) or even a minor annoyance (such as the incessant barking of the neighbor's dog), it's hard to imagine how these challenges reflect our true desires! Yet whenever I look back on the so-called problems in my life, I understand now that they were actually opportunities to create significant change and consequently help me achieve my deepest dreams.

For example, as I mentioned before, the raw food diet saved me from my collection of soggy tissues, fear of cat dander, and my unfortunate reaction to pine trees. Yet, as it turns out, it was much more than just an antidote for my severe allergic rhinitis.

It actually helped me find my life purpose.

Remember when I described my epiphany while working on a massage client? While executing the "perfect" effleurage, I felt subtle energy for the first time. I'm convinced that I was able to feel the Force *because* I was on a raw food diet. I suppose this is why fasting, vegetarian, and raw food diets are used within spiritual traditions to help bring people closer to God. Furthermore, as you know, working with subtle energy turned out to be my life's work! Hence, my allergies were indeed a blessing in disguise—an opportunity to create a career doing what I love.

At any moment, we have the power to turn our roadblocks into building blocks. We can either feel defeated by our problems or we can view them as opportunities to help us further our dreams. No matter how difficult life has been up to this point, it's never too late to transform adversity into abundance.

And how do we do this?

You guessed it.

We invoke the magic of ownership!

We commit to taking full ownership of *everything* in our life.

Now I know what you might be thinking. It's easy to take responsibility for the good stuff, but what about the "not so good" stuff? For example, we can readily pat ourselves on the back for manifesting our dream home, yet it's much harder to own the fact that we "created" an obnoxious neighbor, a flooded bathroom, or an overwhelming tax bill. Can we really accept that fact that *we create everything*—including the good, the bad, and the ugly?

The answer is yes, we *do* create everything (including the pet cat who "accidently" mistakes our expensive Persian rug for kitty litter!). Although it may be challenging, if we can make this ubiquitous shift from victim to owner, our entire life will change for the better. Any change in our vibration or in our energy and essence ripples out into every aspect of our reality. Nothing happens in isolation.

Everything affects everything in miraculous and amazing ways.

In my case, my allergies were actually a magical opportunity to create a life doing what I love. Hence, my "blessing in disguise" taught me a valuable lesson about dreams:

If we don't pursue our dreams, sometimes our dreams will pursue us.

WHY BUDGETS FAIL

A budget tells us what we can't afford,
but it doesn't keep us from buying it.

WILLIAM FEATHER

It's Not Rocket Science!

When I first set out to pay off my debt and save money, I decided to create a budget.

Great idea, right?

I was pretty impressed with myself for *finally* taking ownership of my finances, having proudly eschewed (for the most part) my victim mentality around money. As we discussed earlier, financial alignment is something that *we create*, rather than a by-product of our circumstances, destiny, being a "good" person, or even the will of God. Adopting an ownership mindset is instrumental to turning our finances around — it's the Essential Shift.

In my case, instead of waiting for God, Spirit, or the Universe to fix my money problems, I decided to take a more empowered approach and embrace a tried and true financial strategy: *spend less than you earn*. As much of the popular financial advice suggests, this is the most important secret to building wealth (or even just digging yourself out of debt.) For example, Robert Kiyosaki, author of *Rich Dad, Poor Dad*, wrote, "It's not how much money you make, but how much money you keep." Benjamin Franklin said, "A penny saved is a penny earned." From a purely logical perspective, this advice certainly makes a lot of sense!

It's not rocket science, right?

So, with the same hopeful anticipation as a child on Christmas Eve, I created a budget spreadsheet and vowed to track every dollar I earned and every penny I spent. I diligently updated my spreadsheet each day, applauding myself for my faithful discipline. I was committed to do whatever it took to get my finances under control—including cutting up my credit cards, relinquishing my creature comforts, getting rid of all my worldly possessions, or suffering though the painful and confusing process of cutting back on business expenses. I felt excited about my new debt-free future, optimistic that my negative net worth would soon be a thing of the past!

Unfortunately, my newfound fiscal plan had a few fatal flaws . . .

Flaw #1: No More Toys!

Marcus Cicero, one of Rome's finest orators, extolled the merits of saving money by suggesting that "frugality includes all the other virtues." Despite Cicero's words of wisdom, I had substantial philosophical objections to the supposed virtues of frugality. In my mind, a frugal life was a joyless and miserable existence, full of suffering, deprivation, and starvation. I was deathly afraid that I would eventually end up as a friendless spinster, living in a cold, dark shack full of rats and cobwebs (and in my miserly state, I couldn't even afford a cat to scare off the rats!)

My new budget certainly reinforced my fear of frugality. I had curtailed my expenses dramatically, forcing myself to stick to a strict allowance. Consequently, I felt extremely deprived, as though I were embarking on a misguided, extreme, and painful crash diet. Sure, anyone can lose weight quickly by forcing themselves to follow the latest tortuous, chocolate-free, and drastic weight-loss scheme. Yet, as most of us know, starvation diets tend to produce an equal and opposite reaction: the rapid consumption of ice cream, chocolate, and carbs, causing the lost weight to return with a vengeance! Similarly, I would make a few feeble attempts to reduce my spending, and then, fueled by massive feelings of deprivation, embark on a colossal rebound shopping spree.

Flaw #2: Lack of Willpower

Despite my hesitancy to embrace the merits of frugality, I decided to take what I call the "brute force" approach to money management and cut up all my credit cards. Unfortunately, I had zero success with this new savings plan. Soon after I sliced and diced my beloved Mastercard, Visa, and Macy's card, I sheepishly fished them out of trash and taped them back together. As I put the mangled cards back in my wallet, I felt ashamed of myself, like a guilty dog caught in the act of devouring all the kitty treats. Did I have no self-control?

Why was I so incapable of sticking to a budget?

The truth is, even when I accumulated $135,000 of debt, *I knew I was doing something wrong!* I was very aware that I *should* be spending a lot less money, but I just couldn't do it. Evidently my lack of willpower would always sabotage my financial future.

Flaw #3: Budgets Are Bad for Business

Trying to cut my business expenses was even more disheartening than my misguided attempt to sacrifice my credit cards. For one thing, I could never figure out what to cut! Eliminating even the smallest expense seemed more precarious than gingerly removing the five of spades from a particularly fragile house of cards. Any budget cut had the potential to severely compromise the business, or even cause it to crumble to the ground!

For example, cutting back on our customer service or product quality was unthinkable for me; I couldn't bear the thought of creating unhappy customers. Sacrificing my integrity for money was out of the question. Laying off an employee was equally impossible; it felt just as painful as saying good-bye to a beloved pet or family member. I just didn't have the heart to do it (unless we were in grave and immediate danger of bouncing payroll!) Furthermore, all cost-cutting measures limited our ability to run the business, which ultimately lowered our income, which then required more cuts, which then lowered our income even more . . .

Arrgh!

Newton's Third Law

Have you ever noticed that some people seem to create abundance wherever they go? We often hear stories of famous people who lose everything and then bounce back from the abyss, wealthier than ever. Even during the Great Depression, some people still knew how to make a buck. For example, on August 4, 1930, American entrepreneur Michael J. Cullen opened the world's first supermarket. Within two years, his stores (known as King Kullen Grocery) were doing more than $6 million in revenue despite the price-conscious environment of the Great Depression.

On the other hand, many of us can't seem to get ahead, no matter what we do—even in a booming economy! It's not uncommon for lottery winners to end up with even less than they had before they won their millions. According to multiple studies, about 70 percent of all lottery winners end up filing for bankruptcy. Many of us try to save money only to discover that life gets in the way, and we find ourselves saddled with an unexpected expense, such as large medical bill, uninsured flood damage, or a car that needs a new transmission.

So why is it so easy for some people to make money, yet so difficult for others?

In my case, both my business and personal finances were always operating at a loss, and nothing I did ever seemed to have any impact on the bottom line. Even if I did manage to summon up some willpower and cut my spending, my income would, remarkably and undeniably *decrease* by that same amount. Making more money never made a dent in my debt either. If I did bring in more income, I always had an *unexpected* expense that would eat up all of my extra earnings. For example, if I earned an extra $500, I would then undoubtedly have an unforeseen expense, such as a car repair, a plumbing leak, or something else—totaling, you guessed it, $500!

Strangely enough, my income *always* seemed to magically and precisely match my expenses, no matter what changes I tried to make. My finances were the illustrious exemplification of Newton's Third Law:

For every action, there is an equal and opposite reaction.

Even if I *did* manage to stick to my budget, I still couldn't circumvent the gravity of Newton's Third Law. Clearly more was going on beneath the surface than just a simple math problem involving income and expenses. I was convinced that some unseen, cosmic, mysterious force was working against me—always keeping me spiritual and broke.

What's Wrong with This Picture?

So, why did my attempt to follow a budget fail so miserably? Imagine that you are trying to repair a hole in the living room wall. One way to address the issue is to cover it up with a picture and hope that no one looks behind it.

Believe me, I've "repaired" a few holes this way! However, the best way to fix the problem is to drag out the can of spackle, carefully fill the hole, patiently wait for the spackle to dry, sand the area you just repaired, realize that you didn't wait long enough for the spackle to dry, reapply the spackle, and then eventually repaint the wall. Of course, simply covering the gap is a lot easier, yet in the end, you still have a hole in the wall!

In a similar way, my attempt to create a budget was like trying to cover a gaping hole with a beautiful piece of artwork. I wasn't addressing the *real* reason I was spiritual and broke. The problem wasn't a poorly designed spreadsheet or even a lack of willpower. Instead, as I suspected, there was indeed an enigmatic Force at work, making it impossible for my budget to succeed.

As I discuss throughout this book, everything is energy. You, me, our beloved Schrödinger, and everything else has its own vibrational frequency. Our entire reality—including our bank account—is a reflection of our own energy. If we want to get out of debt, improve our health, or make other long-lasting changes, we first need to shift our vibration. Remember, "match the frequency of the reality you want and you cannot help but get that reality."

My optimistic plan to follow a budget failed because I was trying to force myself to cut my spending without first addressing my vibration around money. As I learned the hard way, if we want to improve our financial situation, we need to transform our energy around money. We need to change our relationship with our finances. In a similar way, we all know that diets don't work (long-term) unless we change our relationship with food. In both cases, getting out of the victim mentality is the essential first step.

The good news is that we *can* create financial alignment without subjecting ourselves to a tedious spreadsheet or unrealistic and painful spending cuts. However, changing our *energetic relationship* with money can be much trickier and less straightforward than simply using logic, creating a spreadsheet, thinking good thoughts, cutting up our credit cards, or trying to embrace the alleged merits of a frugal lifestyle.

First of all, shifting our vibration around money requires an incredible level of self-awareness. As we explored in chapter five, our vibration is the underlying energy and essence of who we are. It encompasses many aspects of our being-ness, including our thoughts, emotions, actions, unconscious and conscious beliefs, unique life path, and purpose. It can be quite an extensive undertaking to comprehend the full energy and essence of who we are as multidimensional beings! Even though I've worked with energy for years, I'm *still* not always fully aware of the energy that I'm projecting out into the world.

Second, finding an *effective* strategy to shift our energy can involve a lot of guesswork, heartbreak, and frustration. What works for one person may not work for another. I know people who have diligently and arduously tried seemingly everything to improve their life, including energy healing, astrology, shamanic journeys, webinars, juice fasting, and every other conceivable technique out there. And yet, much to their disappointment, their long-suffering journey did not produce the results they were hoping for. Other people try a new technique, quickly see results, and then happily move on with their life.

In all my years of working with energy, I have come to the conclusion that there is no "one size fits all" cookie-cutter technique for "vibrational change." Changing our energy around money, relationships, health, or anything else for that matter may seem incredibly daunting because, for most people, the world of energy and vibration isn't necessarily that easy to see, touch, or understand! Shifting our energy can be an *aimless, difficult, haphazard, meandering process of trial and error.*

So how do we know where to start, what to change, or what to do?

In the rest of this book, I show you how to create financial alignment by *shifting your energy,* so that you can tune into the frequency of abundance. It's possible to eliminate debt, build a savings account, and stop struggling with money once and for all—*all without feeling deprived!* Believe me, if I can do it, anyone can!

You have the power to change anything in your life, just by changing yourself.

That's all you need to do.

There is a store house within you from which you can extract everything you need to live life glorious, joyously, abundantly.
JOSEPH MURPHY

DIVINE GUIDANCE

When you don't know what to do, do nothing.
Get quiet so you can hear that still, small voice.

OPRAH WINFREY

Cosmic GPS

I'm the type of person that can get lost in a plain brown paper bag. Before the invention of GPS (Global Positioning System), this trait caused me all sorts of trouble whenever I got behind the wheel. (Those who are "directionally challenged" can probably relate!) I have spent countless evenings aimlessly touring some remote suburb in an unfamiliar city, desperately trying to find the freeway (any freeway, for that matter!). Going someplace new routinely filled me with panic; typically, I would drive for hours trying to find a meeting location, restaurant, or friend's house. Even when I lived in the same place for years and traversed the identical route countless times, I still got lost!

Thankfully, my navigational challenges became a distant memory after I received a GPS device as a gift. I finally had a foolproof way to reach my destination without various unwanted detours along the way. Now when I travel, I actually *enjoy* exploring the area, knowing I'll always find my way back to my hotel. Thanks to my trusty GPS, I no longer show up late for meetings or frantically drive around same unfamiliar neighborhood, trying to find my way home. To me, this little wonder of technology was a godsend.

I've extolled the virtues of the GPS to make a point: if we are navigating a brand-new area or trying to return home on a dark and stormy night, it definitely helps to have a guide! Likewise, it's certainly beneficial to have a Guide when it comes to navigating the world of energy, frequency, and vibration.

As we discussed earlier, everything in our universe is energy. If we want to create real, long-lasting shifts with our money, health, and relationships, we need to shift our energy first and foremost. That's why creating a budget won't improve our finances—unless we first transform our energy around money.

Yet for many of us, shifting our vibration involves a lot of trial and error and here's why. First of all, although each of has the *capacity* to see and perceive energy, some of us may not know *how* to fully tap into our innate ability to do so. (Actually, perhaps I should say that many of us may not *remember* how to utilize our innate ability to sense energy— because I believe that kids and pets tend do this naturally.) Second, even if we can see the world as energy, that doesn't necessarily mean we know how to change it!

Fortunately, there's a solution to this vibrational conundrum!

We all have a Global Vibrational Positioning System— or GVPS, as I like to call it—that helps us navigate the world of energy. Instead of guiding us to Disneyland or the nearest gas station, this cosmic GPS provides us with step-by-step instructions to shift our energy and attract our desired reality. In other words, our GVPS has the ability to show us how to shift our vibration so we can attract more money, better health, or more inspiring relationships. (And unlike a normal GPS, it never goes offline, even in remote areas!) This Global Vibrational Positioning System is the knowledge, wisdom, and guidance that comes from a Divine Source, such as God, Angels, Spirit Guides, or the Universe. It's what I refer to as our *Divine Guidance*.

Now, I know what you're thinking. This whole Divine Guidance idea seems a bit far-fetched, unscientific, or even like complete nonsense—a fairy tale reserved for hippies and zealots. I totally understand! I used to be a skeptic as well. Having a background in computer science, I *love* the idea of taking any problem and reducing it to a tried and true algorithm with clear instructions, precise details for every step, and perhaps even a few mathematical formulas thrown in as well. That's why my attempt to create a budget spreadsheet was so appealing to me; it involved numbers and math equations!

Although the concept of Divine Guidance may seem a bit "out there," I believe that even the most die-hard skeptics have experienced Divine Guidance at some point or another. For example, I have a friend who doesn't believe in spirituality, life after death, angels, God, or anything "New Age." Yet on more than one occasion, he mentioned that his "little voice" saved him from an untimely death or a catastrophic injury. As author Echo Bodine suggests, "I've come to believe, on the journey of mine, that we have a still small voice—and that voice does come from God." I'm convinced that most people have heard their "little voice" at some point, without being aware that it was their GVPS at work.

That was certainly the case for me.

Engineering Personality Disorder

When I was growing up, my mom was forced to share a house with two engineers. My dad was a radio frequency (RF) engineer and I was a software engineer in the making. My mom (poor thing) was convinced that we suffered from what she called "engineering personality disorder" or EPD for short.

EPD is characterized by an excessively analytical approach to life and the inability to appreciate anyone's emotions, including our own! My dad and I had the tendency to take any object or experience and dismantle it into its logical components, unable to just enjoy the moment. Instead, we needed to understand the mathematics *behind* the moment. And heaven forbid if anyone expressed any strong emotions in our family! Both my dad and I immediately labeled them as "illogical" and scratched our heads in bewilderment, unable to navigate the confusing and seemingly unproductive range of human emotion. When dealing with feelings, there was certainly no order, process, or mathematics to rely on!

I used to believe that my EPD served me quite well. I breezed through college, easily graduating magna cum laude with a degree in computer science. I credited my EPD for my successful career as a software developer, believing that any problem could be solved by reducing it to a tried-and-true algorithm. No intellectual puzzle was beyond my reach! I even felt more "evolved" and productive than other people because I based my decisions on logic rather than my seemingly nonsensical emotions.

As the journalist Allen Saunders once said, "Life is what happens to you when you're busy making other plans." Perhaps I could have spent the rest of my life enjoying the benefits of my EPD, but the Universe had something else in mind. My life became a series of synchronistic twists and turns that ultimately convinced even a highly analytical engineer like me to set aside my addiction to logic and listen to my heart.

My fastidious dedication to the virtues of EPD started to fade when I first discovered "the Force" back in massage school. From that day forward, I knew without a doubt energy medicine was my life's work. Shortly after that, I met Richard Gordon, the founder of Quantum-Touch, and I instantly knew that Quantum-Touch was my destiny. Although my rational, logical mind questioned the Guidance I was receiving, *something* compelled me to move forward regardless. I was inspired to take a leap of faith and follow my heart, even though I didn't know what the outcome would be ahead of time. Throughout this journey, I felt that I was being *guided* by the Universe, God, Spirit, or a Force greater than me. I was following what I now believe was my Divine Guidance, even though I wasn't fully aware of it at the time.

My story goes to show that even a "matter-of-fact," skeptical, logical person can have a change of heart and believe in something as "touchy-feely" and enigmatic as

Divine Guidance. I now acknowledge that the answers to life's questions cannot always be reduced to a series of logic and switching circuits. If we were able to merely plug some numbers into a computer and come up with an equation for wealth, weight loss, or happiness, more of us would probably be super thin, multimillionaires, living out our deepest fantasies! Instead, the answers to our prayers often come in magical and mysterious ways, leading us on journeys beyond our imagination and certainly beyond reason.

All we need to do is to let go and follow the divine flow!

Angel Therapy

After I discovered the Force back in massage school, I started following my Divine Guidance, somewhat haphazardly and without a real awareness of what I was doing. The pieces didn't come together until I attended a seminar on Angel Therapy led by Doreen Virtue. She is known as the "the angel lady" and is a prolific writer on topics such as angels, Divine Guidance, fairies, ascended masters, and spirituality. I had been a fan of hers for years, so when I saw that she was teaching on Maui, I quickly grabbed the opportunity to attend her workshop.

During the seminar, one of her assistants shared his own story about Divine Guidance. He had started his career as an accountant, and although his job paid the bills, he knew he wasn't living his purpose. Instead, he felt called to start offering intuitive guidance in the form of angel readings. After some soul-searching, he took a leap of faith, quit his job, and tried to make a living doing Angel Therapy. He thought he was doing the right thing, yet he completely failed to pay the bills and put food on the table!

Even though he returned to his job as an accountant, he still felt compelled to follow his true calling. So he quit his job for the *second* time and again attempted to pursue a career in Angel Therapy. This time he was incredibly successful at it, even co-authoring books with Doreen Virtue.

Why was the second time the charm?

What he said next was an "Aha!" moment for me. The first time he quit his job, he tried to make his Angel Therapy business work by using a strictly logical approach business building. After quitting his job for the second time, he actually *followed* his Divine Guidance. His story made me realize that I had been following my own Divine Guidance mostly by accident and certainly not on a consistent basis. However, when I did manage to follow my Divine Guidance, I noticed, just like Doreen Virtue's assistant, that things tended to work out and flow much better.

Are You There, God?

In December 2004, a catastrophic tsunami hit the shores of Thailand, claiming almost 300 thousand lives. Despite the enormity of human casualties, very few animals died. Before the giant waves slammed into the coastline, both wild and domestic animals sensed imminent danger and fled to safety. In Bang Koey, a herd of buffalo suddenly lifted their heads and looked out toward the sea, ears standing in upright military fashion, and then they all turned and stampeded up the hill. At Ao Sane beach near Phuket, dogs were seen running to higher ground. Flamingos abandoned their low-lying breeding areas, and zoo animals rushed into their shelters. Somehow all of these animals sensed that a tsunami was coming!

How did they know?

History is chock-full of stories about animals who have acted in what we perceive as strange and unusual ways right before a natural disaster. Most scientists agree that it is possible for animals to sense changes in the environment before humans do. Yet there has been no conclusive evidence as to how animals are able to do this! One explanation is that animals sense the earth's vibrations. Another is that they can detect changes in the air or gasses released by the earth.

I have a different theory, however . . .

I believe that animals naturally follow their Divine Guidance at all times. During the Thailand tsunami, very few animals lost their lives because their still small voice warned them of imminent danger. Their Divine Guidance urged them to flee to higher ground, precisely at the right time.

Likewise, we constantly see evidence that our pets are tuned into their Higher Wisdom. For example, dogs mysteriously know *exactly* when their owners are returning home, even at unexpected times. A cat will suddenly jolt awake from a sound sleep and race to the kitchen, keenly aware that it's dinnertime. Yet that same attentive and affectionate feline will completely disappear when it's time to go to the vet (even before the cat carrier comes out). And there are many stories of "seizure alert dogs" that can alert their owners of an oncoming epileptic attack minutes before it occurs.

The way I see it, all animals—kittens and elephants alike—are tuned into the cosmic GPS. Furthermore, this ability to "tune in" isn't just limited to pets and wild buffalo; we each have the capacity to connect to our own Divine Guidance at any time.

In fact, it's our birthright!

Just like the flamingos in Thailand, we all have the power to sense an impending natural disaster. We all have the intuitive ability to know when danger lies ahead or someone is telling a lie. Like our pets, we all have the ability to predict when a loved one is coming home. We even have the capability to foresee which stocks will perform the best or "tune into" a fortuitous connection that leads us to a prosperous new opportunity. In essence, when it comes to making an important decision, our Divine Guidance is one of our most powerful assets!

So, if listening to our Divine Guidance is really that beneficial, *why doesn't everyone do it?*

The Still Small Voice

"If we all could see the world through the eyes of a child,
we would see the magic in everything."
CHEE VAI TANG

Let's face it, our Divine Guidance can be really challenging to hear! Even though I've written an entire chapter on Divine Guidance, I *still* have trouble hearing my own Guidance at times. In fact, it seems like I have more trouble hearing my Guidance when I actually need it the most. When I'm feeling heartbroken, alienated, angry, or depressed, it feels like my Guidance is nowhere to be found.

Can you relate?

Wouldn't it be convenient if our Divine Guidance worked like the GPS on our phone? We could just go to our "GVPS App," enter in our problems, hopes, fears, and dreams, and it would provide loud, clear, audible, and foolproof directions on what to do next. We could select "meet my soul mate" as our desired destination and our special GVPS would promptly provide us with step-by-step instructions, leading us to the exact location of our true love: merge onto US-111 S; in seven miles take the Merry Lane Rd. exit, EXIT 77; the love of your life lives in the seventh house on the right.

Then we all could then live happily ever after!

Right?

Well, Divine Guidance doesn't quite work that way.

First of all, unlike a "traditional GPS," Divine Guidance doesn't strictly adhere to Dijkstra's "shortest path" algorithm. It won't blindly tell us to turn down an unpaved, unlit dirt road in the middle of the night just because it's the shortest distance to our destination (unless that particular route is actually the most effective way to manifest our heart's desire).

Second, our GVPS doesn't necessarily speak to us using an audible voice (with perhaps an alluring British or Australian accent). Our Divine Guidance may not come to us in words at all, and if it does, it can be significantly more subtle than voice navigation.

Although it may not always feel like it, our Divine Guidance is always available to us. The cosmic GPS is a lot like the radio waves that are constantly buzzing through the air. When we select a particular channel on the radio, we hear a specific type of music, news, or commercials. If we are between channels, we hear random noise or dead air. In the same way, Divine Guidance is perpetually at our disposal, hovering in the cosmic airwaves 24/7, even at 3:00 a.m. The biblical principle, "Ask and you shall receive," is true. All the answers are accessible to us, right at this very moment. Everyone, animals and humans alike, is innately wired to hear their Divine Guidance.

All we need to do is tune in.

What's more, we already have everything we need to do so! Our heart acts like a special radio receiver that can tune into the cosmic GPS anytime we want. The secret to hearing Divine Guidance is to listen with an open heart.

Sounds simple, right?

In fact, it's so simple that animals and children do it naturally. They instinctively approach life with their hearts fully open. When we look into their eyes, we know exactly what is in their heart. If an animal or child is happy, hurting, angry, or excited, we understand without a doubt how they feel. For example, when a dog rapidly wags his tail, we know that he's excited to see us; we can easily tell the difference between a "playful meow" and a "forlorn meow;" and mothers readily notice the subtle emotional nuances of their baby's cries.

Each of us is born with our hearts fully open, completely in tune with our GVPS. Yet as we grow older, many of us tend to lose touch with that still, small voice of the heart, and Divine Guidance no longer flows naturally to us.

Here's why, as I see it . . .

First of all, our society in general discourages us from listening to our heart. The majority of our institutions—such as the military, stock market, legal system, corporate world, and educational system—seem to reward us for setting aside our feelings so we can be more productive and efficient. We are often encouraged to ignore the heart and listen to the mind. This isn't necessarily a bad thing when it comes to building a road, solving a quadratic equation, or understanding Dijkstra's algorithm. However, ignoring the heart also makes it extremely difficult to hear our Divine Guidance.

Second, as a result of our collective emphasis on rational thought, many people go great lengths to suppress their true, authentic feelings. For example, many of us feel ashamed when we cry, and try to hide our tears in embarrassment or apologize for "making a scene." We pretend we don't feel hurt or angry when we actually do. Men especially are programmed, through years of practice, to dismiss their emotions. How many times have we heard the phrases "suck it up" or "be a man"? It's no wonder why lots of people eat "comfort foods," take up smoking, drink copious amounts of wine, binge-watch TV, or become workaholics in an attempt to numb their painful emotions. I personally can attest to the fact that a large bar of chocolate will solve all of my problems (a least for an hour or so)!

Finally, as the famous singer Tina Turner once declared, "Who needs a heart if a heart can be broken?" As a response to trauma and tragedy, we tend to build protective walls around our heart. Who could blame us? It's perfectly natural to shut down as an attempt to shield ourselves from heartbreak and sorrow. When I'm feeling grief-stricken, hurt, violated, or betrayed, all I want to do is safeguard my heart and fantasize about moving to an uninhabited island. The last thing I want to do is open my heart!

Although it may be tempting to ignore our feelings, closing our heart also has the unfortunate side effect of shutting down our GVPS—which ironically is the very thing we need to keep us safe! Divine Guidance is incredibly proficient at protecting us from heartbreak, danger, and pain, while guiding us toward what we truly want. It can warn us of an impending natural disaster, prevent us from marrying the wrong person, block us from boarding an ill-fated plane, and help us adopt the perfect kitten.

So, how do we open our heart after years of emotional suppression, tragedy, trauma, and heartbreak?

Doesn't it require years of intense therapy?

Or copious amounts of spiritual healing?

Or perhaps a near-death experience?

How do we hear our Divine Guidance, even if our heart is completely shut down?

A Faint Light in the Fog

"Gratitude opens your heart, and opening your heart is a wonderful and easy way for God to slip in."
RAM DASS

Have you ever been tempted to run off and join the circus? I actually did!

Well, sort of . . .

I discovered the flying trapeze when I moved to Los Angeles, California, in 2008, and I absolutely loved it! In fact, the flying trapeze was largely responsible for my move to Maui in 2013. A new flying trapeze school had just opened up on the island, and my love for Hawaii combined with my passion for the circus compelled me to make the move. Taking that death-defying leap to fly through the air required me to be fully present in the moment and forget everything else. And practicing full mindfulness is good for our health. As Buddha suggests, the secret of health for both mind and body is "to live the present moment wisely and earnestly."

After that horrible night when an intruder broke into my house, I found an incredible amount of solace in the flying trapeze. It was an opportunity to set aside my grief and anger and just have fun, at least for a little while. So you can image my devastation, when two years after I moved to Maui, my beloved flying trapeze school closed. I couldn't "fly" anymore and felt myself slipping into a deep depression. I was still facing the emotional fallout from that terrible night, and now I no longer had my circus community and my respite from the world. I had lost "my saving grace."

At that time, I was renting a home on Maui that was rather charming, except that it had a big pile of dirt for a yard. Since I had always dreamed of living next to a tropical garden oasis (not a bunch of dust and weeds), I decided to turn my landlord's dilapidated dirt mound into a beautiful garden. I spent hours out in the yard, planting flowers, pulling weeds, cultivating newly planted grass, and creating a beautiful landscape.

Much to my delight, the garden took on a life of its own! It was always changing in enchanting ways; flowers magically appeared overnight, grass slowly replaced the dirt, and butterflies and bees moved in. I developed a newfound appreciation for the exquisite and delicate complexity of a flower and the breathtaking smell of a plumeria tree.

Although I was disheartened and upset most of the time,

I couldn't help but feel a moment of gratitude and wonder for my burgeoning garden, the beauty of nature, myself, God, and all of life itself. In these breathtaking yet fleeting moments, I began to notice that I could actually hear the still small voice of my heart. My brief moments of appreciation opened the doorway to my heart and my Divine Guidance was right there quietly waiting for me.

My Divine Guidance certainly had a lot to say! In fact, it urged me to write a book. As I continued to cultivate my garden, I received an astonishing amount of information about this new book, including the title, the chapters, the content, and even the size of the book! Suddenly I had a renewed purpose in life. My anger and grief started to fade as I embarked on an inspiring new journey—this time as an author. In 2016 I published my first book, *Love Incorporated: The Business of Doing What You Love.*

When I first started working on my garden, I initially intended to cultivate a beautiful landscape. What I didn't expect is how much my garden would cultivate me! It taught me an invaluable lesson:

The key to opening the heart is gratitude.

I know how seemingly impossible it can be to summon up any sort of appreciation for life when it feels like everything sucks, you're going through a divorce, you can't pay your bills, your cat disappears, or you're recovering from a major trauma such as the loss of a child or a horrible crime.

Believe me, I get it!

However, even when everything seems to be falling apart,

we can *still* find our gratitude, no matter what. All we need to do is spend some time each day doing something that we love.

Now, gardening may not be for everyone, but everyone can find *something* they love to do. Perhaps you enjoy riding your bike, savoring a wonderful dinner, jumping on a trampoline, or listening to uplifting music. Some people use meditation, fasting, or yoga as tools to open their heart. By now you know that few things open my heart more than the beauty of nature or the purr of a happy cat! The point is, we just need to do whatever it takes, consistently each day, to actually be present and *feel* our love, gratitude, and joy, even if it's just for a little while. Once we arrive at that place inside, we are automatically tuned into our Divine Messages.

Even if we've spent a lifetime burying our heart beneath layers of suppressed emotion, fear, alienation, and pain, we are never far away from that still small voice. Like a faint light in the fog, the heart is always there, steadfastly guiding us home. If we can crack open the door, even for just a little while, we will find our Divine Guidance patiently waiting for us.

Divine Guidance really wants to speak to us.

All we need is an open heart.

And a little bit of faith.

For truly, I say to you, if you have faith like a grain of mustard seed, you will say to this mountain, "Move from here to there," and it will move, and nothing will be impossible for you.

JESUS CHRIST

Guidance versus Mind Chatter

If you're anything like me, your mind is constantly bombarding you with suggestions, ideas, longings, fantasies, mental images, and even what appears to be some sort of guidance from time to time:

I would love to get married someday.
Don't go the store after 10:00 p.m. or you might get robbed.
What if my house catches on fire in the middle of the night?
Maybe I shouldn't board that plane . . .
Life would be better if I lost ten pounds!

So, the question is, how do we differentiate true Divine Guidance from the random and sometimes disempowering musings of the mind?

First of all, the still small voice *feels* very different than our "normal" thoughts. It is *always* loving, supportive, and inspirational, even when it is warning us of impending danger. On the other hand, random mind chatter tends to feel negative, judgmental, fearful, and disempowering. For example, our Divine Guidance may gently advise us to gather our belongings and evacuate our house because a hurricane is on the way. The mind, on the other hand, will encourage us to live in constant fear of hurricanes, tsunamis, floods, and fires.

Second, true Divine Guidance is *always* consistent, whereas the mind can be incredibly fickle. Our mind may advise us to move to California, and then a day later suggest relocating to New York. In contrast, Divine Guidance will repeat the same message over and over again (sometimes, annoyingly, for years!) until we take action.

Third, Divine Guidance offers us direction in an empowering, objective, and unbiased way, even if it's advice about self-improvement. In contrast, the mind often inflicts harsh criticism on ourselves and others. For example, the mind can be our own worst critic: "Geez, I'm looking incredibly ugly and fat today. No wonder I can't get a date." On the other hand, the cosmic GPS will guide us in a positive and loving way: "It's time to eat healthier food (and in the process, you may lose weight)." Furthermore, true Divine Guidance doesn't judge others. It would never suggest that "Sheila's new purple dress is wildly inappropriate for the office" or "Tom is a narcissist." However, our Divine Guidance may advise us to refrain from creating a business contract with Tom (without judging Tom's psychological profile).

Finally, the still small voice is constantly urging us to follow our heart and be authentic, whereas the mind tends to emphasize our fears and actually discourages us from living our purpose. The heart says, "Give it a try," while the mind says, "I'll never succeed." The heart says, "Embrace your dreams," while the head says, "We'll never achieve our dreams, so we might as well settle for the practical choice." The heart says, "Do what you love," while the mind says, "I no longer believe in fairy tales!" The heart says, "Remember that book you always dreamed about writing? Let's get started!" while the mind says, "Your book is a waste of time. Don't even try!" The heart says, "I would love to be a teacher," and the mind says, "Being a teacher doesn't pay very much."

Our Divine Guidance always aligns with our true values, hope, dreams, and life purpose.

It empowers, encourages, and inspires us.

It resonates with our greatest joy.

It's the voice of our authentic self.

It always feels like Truth.

Follow your instincts. That's where
true wisdom manifests itself.
OPRAH WINFREY

You Want Me to Do What? (Following Our Guidance)

Often the greatest obstacle between a person and their goals is themselves.
AUTHOR UNKNOWN

I have a confession to make . . . Sometimes I *ignore* my Divine Guidance. Every now and then, I hear that still small voice of the heart and then promptly disregard it.

Now, I'm sure you may be wondering, if I ignore my Divine Guidance, why would I go through all the effort to tune into it in the first place?

That's a great question!

Here's why: Following our Divine Guidance may not always be very easy, fun, or painless. Often our GVPS will point us in a direction that is scary, difficult, unbelievable, seemingly impractical, potentially fraught with naysayers, and terribly uncomfortable! How many times has the still small voice urged us to give up an addiction, leave an unhealthy relationship, move to a new place, or forgive someone we don't want to forgive? We may receive our Divine Guidance loud and clear—yet taking action can be another story altogether!

However, it's not easy to avoid that still small voice for long. It can be more persistent than an enthusiastic, hyperactive puppy that constantly wants to play. Ignoring Divine Guidance, particularly over time, can have some seriously unpleasant consequences (perhaps we could call them "growth opportunities"). I have countless stories that illustrate just how bad things became when I didn't listen to my still small voice.

One of my most bemusing stories ever involves the time I ignored my Divine Guidance and ended up in a house full of rats and sewage!

Here's what happened . . .

When I was a child, I used to love the 1970's TV commercials for C & H Pure Cane Sugar because they enchanted me with their idyllic portrayal of life in Hawaii. Children smiled and laughed as they ran through radiant, tall sugarcane grasses. Puppies innocently played in the bright Hawaiian sunshine. Families walked along the warm, gleaming beaches holding hands. Even back then, I knew I wanted to live in Hawaii; it was my perfect, charming, and magical home!

When I was thirty, my childhood dream came true: I moved to Maui, Hawaii. I felt in my heart that I was finally home where I belonged. However, strangely enough, I didn't stay home for long. Two years later I moved back to California to embark on my new journey as the CEO of Quantum-Touch. And over the next twelve years, I moved back and forth between Hawaii and the mainland USA *seven times*.

Now, relocating across the Pacific Ocean is quite an ordeal. We can't just rent a truck, pack up our possessions, and drive to our next destination. Instead we have to haul all our stuff to the nearest harbor, put everything on a boat, and then patiently wait until our belongings arrive in Hawaii. On top of that, it's incredibly expensive to ship everything to an island that's over 3,000 miles away from the closest continental land mass.

Given the time, expense, and inconvenience of moving to Hawaii, you may be wondering why I moved seven times.

Was I just plain insane?

Actually, I was tremendously indecisive. I felt horribly torn between my heart and my head. On one hand, living in California seemed to be the practical choice for myself and Quantum-Touch. After all, the mainland has more resources than Hawaii, including commercial space, office supplies, the latest technology, and an incredible amount of business opportunities. On the other hand, my heart always craved Hawaii. That's why my inner battle between head and heart resulted in numerous and expensive treks across the Pacific Ocean.

My geographic vacillation finally came to an end after I moved back to California for the sixth time. Even though I had always felt guided to stay in Hawaii, I tried yet again to make California my home. While steadfastly ignoring my inner voice, I forced myself to power through a difficult and frustrating search for housing. I finally ended up renting what appeared to be a pleasant place in Topanga.

Unfortunately, my new home wasn't as delightful as I thought it would be. The day I moved in, I noticed a funny odor in the master bedroom. I brushed it off, thinking that perhaps the previous tenant had owned a dog. Convinced that the smell would soon dissipate, I decided to end a long, stressful day of moving with a lovely soak in the tub. As I was getting ready to unwind, I made a horrifying discovery. The odd smell wasn't due to a former pet. Instead, it was caused by something far worse: my new home was infested with rats, some of which lived under the tub. Needless to say, my relaxing bath never happened.

Instead of calling the local moving company, (which is what I should have done), I contacted a local eco-friendly pest control company. Over a period of several weeks, they removed the rats, cleaned the attic, and patched up holes in the house to prevent future rat infestations. After the rodent clean-up was complete, I thought my troubles were over.

Wrong!

Much to my horror, my domestic problems continued. Soon after the rats moved out, raw sewage started spewing out from the toilet in the downstairs bathroom! Shortly after this nasty plumbing fiasco, I woke up to a "rotten egg" smell coming from the kitchen. As it turned out, the house had multiple gas leaks. My nightmare continued when I came home late one night and found the front door wide open! Apparently, the locks randomly stopped working for no reason. On top of that, the heater stopped working in the middle of winter.

After spending a lot of time, energy, and money trying to convert my ill-fated rental into a livable home, I eventually waved the white flag and surrendered to the still small voice. I decided to follow my heart, and I moved to Hawaii for the last time. I was finally home for good.

My disastrous, rat-infested, sewage-spewing rental taught me a very important lesson about Divine Guidance. If we ignore the still small voice of the heart, it doesn't just go away. Our circumstances are *always* co-conspiring to lead us toward our authentic truth. Initially, the Universe will *gently* guide us in the direction of our heart's desire. And then, for stubborn people like me, the nudges will become louder and louder, stronger and stronger, until we come face-to-face with rats and sewage and we finally acquiesce to that still small voice.

Remember the old saying, "A stitch in time saves nine?" It certainly applies to Divine Guidance! As I learned the hard way, it's better to follow our Divine Guidance right away rather than wait until a disaster happens!

And who knows where Divine Guidance will lead?

We just might end up in paradise, enjoying the sugarcane, and living the life of our dreams!

Your heart knows things that your mind can't explain.
KUSHANDWIZDOM

What Matters Most

You'll never see a U-Haul behind a hearse . . ." This poignant and funny remark by the Academy Award-winning actor Denzel Washington has a way of putting our priorities into perspective, doesn't it? As he said, "I can't take it with me and neither can you." When we take our final breath, we leave behind everything we ever cared about on planet earth: house, money, cars, loved ones, businesses, pets. We can't take anything with us—except our love.

Most of us can probably remember at least one time in our life when our heart overflowed with unconditional love. Perhaps we felt a moment of deep gratitude when connecting with a loved one or gazing into our newborn's eyes. Maybe we experienced an overwhelming feeling of adoration for a kitten or a puppy. Perhaps we had a moment of glorious lucidity when admiring the wonderous beauty of a flower. Maybe we gave a gift to someone in need and in return felt a breathtaking sense of pure divine joy. In the end, what truly matters in life are these moments of unconditional love.

Ultimately, the essence of who we are—our authenticity, love, truth, and gratitude—are more valuable than all of the money in the world. So, it makes sense that the cosmic GPS always guides us to follow our heart. Often what we perceive as "negative" circumstances are actually messages from the Universe urging us toward our true heartfelt dreams. Every challenge in life, including money problems, raw sewage and rats, is be an opportunity to open our heart.

In the end, only one question really matters:

Can we find the love in every situation?

> *It matters not*
> *who you love*
> *where you love*
> *when you love*
> *or how you love . . .*
> *It matters only that you love.*
> JOHN LENNON

THE MAGIC OF SIMPLICITY

*The ability to simplify means to eliminate the
unnecessary so that the necessary may speak.*

HANS HOFMANN

A Wrinkle in Time

I t was a dark and stormy night . . ." So begins one of my best-loved books of all time: *A Wrinkle in Time*. The author, Madeleine L'Engle, introduces us to a supernatural universe, whereby people travel to a land far, far away by "wrinkling time," or folding the fabric of space and time, thus creating a magical and convenient shortcut from point A to point B. In this mystical world, the shortest distance between two points is not always necessarily a straight line.

When I first read the book, I was fascinated by the idea of "wrinkling time" in the same way I was captivated by unicorns and fairies; it was a wonderful fantasy, but surely it didn't apply to real life. As I mentioned before, I had always prided myself in taking the most pedantic and practical approach to any problem, believing that it was indeed the most efficient resolution.

In the "real world," there are no shortcuts, right?

However, my Divine Guidance threw a giant monkey wrench into my idealization and dependence on intellectual reason. As I discovered, the cosmic GPS doesn't automatically guide us down the most obvious and linear path. Instead, following Divine Guidance can be a lot like a wrinkle in time: a straight line is not necessarily the most effective way to reach our destination!

Curious Advice

When it comes to Divine Guidance, author Boris Paternak sums up my feelings quite well: "Surprise is the greatest gift which life can grant us." Even though I had asked my Divine Guidance for financial help, much to my surprise, it didn't encourage me to read *Frugal Living for Dummies*, give me stock tips, or even offer effective ways to cut my business spending. Instead it urged me to do something a bit odd and seemingly totally random:

Simplify my life.

Clean out the clutter in my home and business.

Upon hearing this curious advice, I couldn't help but question the sanity of my GVPS. Wasn't my life fairly simple already? Clutter? What clutter?

Surely, this Divine Guidance didn't apply to me! Any stranger visiting my house would have bowed in quiet appreciation, marveling at the conspicuous *lack* of stuff laying around. I was the absolute antithesis of a hoarder. No one had to maneuver around old newspapers, dirty laundry, dead mice, rotting food, ancient paperwork, or towering stacks of books just to get to the bathroom. My closets were *not* filled to the brim with clothes, games, old notes from ex-boyfriends, and my fifth-grade report cards. Rather, I was the type of neat-freak that kept the house so meticulously clean that you could actually eat off the floor, for real!

More importantly, even if I did manage to find some

latent clutter, this Divine Guidance seemed completed un-related to getting out of debt. I was suspicious. How would simplifying my life fix my money problems?

What the heck was my Divine Guidance talking about?

Nevertheless, my cosmic GPS was all too quick to point out that, despite how tidy my home *may* have appeared, I really did have a lot of clutter; it just wasn't visible to the casual observer. For example, our business fileserver con-tained an impossible and disorganized jumble of computer files. I had thousands of ancient emails awaiting my atten-tion with the hope that I would get to them "someday." My overflowing filing cabinets were stuffed with out-of-date paperwork and ten-year-old invoices. I had piles upon piles of bank statements that I seldom looked at because I was always too busy. Furthermore, even though my closets weren't filled to the brim with random stuff, there was still a lot of room for improvement. I owned an assortment of long-forgotten dresses, skirts, blouses, jeans, and sweaters—many of which I never wore. Some outfits still had price tags on them!

Time to face reality.

My life was not as simple or clutter-free as I wanted to believe.

Furthermore, I knew without a doubt that I was indeed hearing my Divine Guidance. The voice of the Universe remained steadfast, never wavering. Like a broken record, it repeated the same thing, over and over again:

Eliminate everything you don't use, and organize the rest.

Rearranging the Deck Chairs

Even though I felt oddly inspired by the divine directive to simplify my life, I still remained skeptical. Cleaning out the clutter seemed just about as productive as rearranging the deck chairs on a sinking Titanic. When our finances are failing, we should plug the gaping holes, not de-clutter our closets, emails, and files . . . right?

However, up until then, I had failed to patch the critical leaks in my financial Titanic, and my ship was sinking fast. Given that I had maxed out my credit cards, was always stressed about money, and couldn't escape the gravity of Newton's Third Law, I figured I had nothing to lose at this point. If my Titanic was going down, I might as well enjoy organizing the deck furniture before its inevitable demise! At the very least, I would revel in the satisfaction of having a clean in-box.

And so, I dutifully embarked on a massive cleaning spree.

Hidden Treasure

I began my quest for simplicity by cleaning out my bedroom closet. I pulled out all my clothes, shoes, games, and keepsakes and sorted through it all, effortlessly filling up a big bag of stuff I never used. I said good-bye to the sweater with the hole in it, the game of Clue I hadn't played in ten years, the brand-new skirt I had never worn, and all the shoes that didn't quite fit. I felt like Santa Claus as I proudly carted off multiple bags of stuff to Goodwill.

Although the local thrift store appreciated my generous donation, my internal naysayer remained skeptical. On one hand, I loved the feeling of letting go; I felt noticeably lighter, as though I had eliminated old, stagnant energy from a part of my life. On the other hand, I didn't understand how organizing a closet would fix my negative net worth.

In fact, what if my quest for simplicity actually made things worse?

I had just spent an entire day organizing my closet, rather than focusing on my failing business! That seemed like a very bad idea.

However, my Divine Guidance persisted, apparently immune to the protests of my inner critic. With unflappable (and annoying) certainty, it advised me to continue the mission to de-clutter my life.

I then turned my attention to something I had been procrastinating on for years: organizing our Quantum-Touch online data. We owned a sophisticated physical computer fileserver which stored all our digital files in a central location, allowing our employees to share documents. Sadly, it was a complete mess. Over the span of many years, we had accumulated gigabytes of outdated files, all strewn haphazardly about. Logging onto our shared network would strike fear into the heart of even the most resilient team members, forcing them to embark on a long-suffering digital treasure hunt just to find the right file.

Given the monstrosity of the task, it took me several months of intense and tedious daily work to clean out our chaotic array of digital information. After deleting a lot of obsolete data, I realized just how few files we actually used on a regular basis. This led me to wonder why we had such a fancy physical fileserver in the first place. Fueled by this new awareness, I migrated our data to a virtual fileserver, which was 90 percent less expensive than our old platform! Furthermore, it was significantly more convenient and easier to use. In fact, our employees loved it! It's a rare and wonderful thing in business when a cost–cutting measure actually makes the team happier.

My next order of business was to de-clutter my physical files. I went through each filing cabinet one by one and shredded all of our antiquated vendor, employee, and banking files. During this process, I ran across a mystery file. It appeared that we had been consistently paying a monthly invoice to an unknown vendor. I quietly wrote the check every month without really giving it much thought, trusting that the bill had some crucial purpose in our company. However, after some research, I discovered that we were still paying for internet service at a property we had vacated *five years ago*. Needless to say, I cancelled the account, and we saved $600 a year.

Now, $600 may not seem like a lot of money. In fact, previously, I had never given this bill a second glance, standing by my belief in author Richard Carlson's decree: "Don't sweat the small stuff." However, small amounts here and there actually add up to quite a lot of money! My haphazard attitude toward paying a small invoice was a symptom of the overload of information and clutter in my life; I simply didn't have the time or energy to deal with it all. However, as I continued to de-clutter my life, I found a lot of extraneous expenses hidden in the "small stuff."

Next, I turned my attention to the large storage unit we were renting for Quantum-Touch. I justified its existence because, in my mind, we needed a place to store our inactive files, which we were required by law to keep for seven years. I also told myself that "someday" I would use all of that random stuff carefully locked away, which included two broken lamps, an ancient postage meter, long-forgotten artwork, a lopsided king-sized mattress, filing cabinets, and a random collection of office supplies. I had a hard time parting with these rarely used but supposedly invaluable possessions. However, when I did the math, I calculated that I could replace everything in the unit if I saved just one year of storage costs. So, I closed the storage unit, saying good-bye to almost everything in it. For the files that we were required to keep, I found a document storage company that specialized in archiving physical files—a service that was *seven times less expensive* than our storage unit!

The divine directive to simplify my life was starting to make sense! At first, I didn't understand why my GVPS was guiding me in that direction. Like a fearful captain, I had nervously steered my Titanic into uncharted waters, cynically anticipating my financial demise. However, I felt pleasantly surprised by what I discovered instead:

Hidden treasure!

I had unearthed an assortment of wayward jewels, *hidden in plain sight*, buried within my previously unexamined collection of clutter. Simplifying my life was like a wrinkle in time, an effective way to cut expenses naturally, without pain, suffering, or impossible decisions. I never felt like I was toying with a fragile house of cards by denying my business something that was essential to its survival. I didn't have to make a heart-wrenching decision to lay off a single mom or cut infrastructure spending. I merely eliminated the unnecessary and counterproductive burdens buried beneath mounds of clutter.

Overall, I had managed to cut some significant expenses *without any feelings of deprivation*. My internal naysayer had become a believer. As the Dalai Lama once said, "The Universe works in mysterious ways."

Speaking of mysterious ways, my continued quest for simplicity exposed a rather mysterious habit: I was spending a lot of money on stuff I rarely used.

The question is, why?

Gazingus Pins

When I began cleaning out my closets, dresser drawers, and garage, I discovered how much I love throw pillows. I collected them the same way some people collect commemorative spoons. My pillow ensemble contained an assorted array of pale blue pillows, ivory pillows, cream pillows, white pillows, butterfly pillows, faux fur pillows, and pillows with beads and sparkles—all in various shapes and sizes, from a classic twenty-six inch "Euro" square pillow to a quaint round pillow, and every conceivable configuration in between. No one, except perhaps Pottery Barn, would question the fact that I had more throw pillows than any normal person could possibly use. My couch and bed were piled high with these decorative pillows, yet I still had more of them hiding in my closet, some of which were still tightly sealed in their original packaging!

Clearly, I was a "throw pillow hoarder"!

I had a similar relationship with makeup. My bathroom cabinets contained a sizeable selection of failed cosmetic experiments: foundation that gave my face a ghostly hue, blush that made me look like a clown, eyeshadow that didn't go with my skin tone, and several expensive lipsticks I had only worn once. I constantly bought makeup in the hopes that *someday* I would discover the exact combination of blush, foundation, and eyeshadow that would land me on the cover of *Vogue*. However, when I contemplated my mostly unused and high-priced collection of lipstick and eyeliner, I had to admit that I rarely used it. Truth be told, I didn't even *enjoy* wearing makeup!

I also possessed enough bath towels for a family of ten, multiple copies of the exact same duvet cover, and countless brand-new sheet sets. Although I certainly wasn't a traditional "hoarder" by any stretch of the imagination, I *did* own a superfluous and expensive collection of certain objects.

I know I'm not the only person on earth with a spending weakness. In fact, there's even a name for it! Vicki Robin and Joe Dominguez, authors of *Your Money or Your Life*, coined the term *gazingus pin* to refer to that item you habitually spend money on, even if you don't need it or even want it. It's something you purchase on autopilot, without really giving it a second thought, even if you already have far more than you need. Most likely, everyone has a few gazingus pins. For example, some people can't resist buying new shoes or sweaters. Others keep collecting electronics, pen, or tools. Or perhaps someone's gazingus pin is a handsome yacht that quietly sits unused, floating in the harbor.

My insatiable appetite for foundation, throw pillows, and duvet covers prompted me to do some soul-searching. Given that I was *already* struggling with money, why did I want to spend *more money* on things I would *never use*?

Did I buy something because it *brought me joy*?

Or was I driven by some other agenda?

When it came to my vast collection of unused makeup, I believed that I was *supposed to wear* makeup because no professional, forty-something year-old woman should ever leave the house without makeup. My makeup collection was strictly the product of my desire to fit in, *rather than something I actually enjoyed*. Likewise, all of my other gazingus pins had similar emotional origins. For example, my throw pillow obsession was a symptom of my longing for people to appreciate my beautiful home. My desire for another blouse, dress, or sweater also stemmed from my craving for the praise and respect of others (especially men). Ultimately, I was spending a lot of money on my misguided attempt to win the approval of others.

Facing the truth behind my gazingus pins was liberating. I realized that buying yet another blouse or bottle of foundation would never eradicate my feelings of unworthiness or satisfy my desire to feel loved. Consequently, I stopped mindlessly spending money on things I didn't need, use, or enjoy—I naturally curtailed my spending, without feeling deprived. Overall, I was very happy with my newfound power over my gratuitous spending habits.

However, I had one gazingus pin that was particularly difficult to face . . .

The Guest Room

"They're sharing a drink called loneliness.
But it's better than drinking alone."
BILLY JOEL, "PIANO MAN"

For years, I had always made a point to only rent homes with enough space for a guest room. I loved the idea of having a lot of visitors and longed for a life filled with friends and laughter. I was somehow under the impression that a guest room was the solution to my loneliness and my ticket to fulfilling relationships. *I even went so far as to rent an extra apartment, at one point, just for friends!*

Much to my dismay, however, very few people actually used my guest room. It often remained empty, taunting me, reminding me of its quiet vacancy. Clearly, a spare room was *not* the answer my feelings of loneliness. I was paying a lot of money to support my dream of having a houseful of loving friends—a fantasy that elevated my housing costs unnecessarily. At one point I was spending about 55 percent of my income on housing!

So, after a "come to Jesus" moment involving an honest assessment of my *actual* housing needs, I moved to a smaller, less expensive place, *without* a guest room. I told myself: "Hey, if I'm going to be lonely, I might as well do so in a place I can afford!" Now I actually use *every room* on a daily basis, even when I'm alone! And I never really felt deprived without a guest room. It really served no purpose other than acting as my make-believe emotional security blanket. In fact, after cutting my housing costs, my lifestyle actually improved; I spent less time cleaning the house or worrying about how I was going to afford it!

As we all know, housing costs have the potential to eat up a lot of our income. Yet cutting back may seem nearly impossible. What if we have a big family and need a larger home? Or we vehemently hate moving? Or we live in Los Angeles, Hawaii, or New York where housing is expensive? Or our spouse and kids would be heartbroken to move? Or we have pets?

I totally get it!

Yet I believe there is a perfect home for each of us,

somewhere in the world, that is affordable *and* enjoyable. Although I personally can't tell you how to find it, I can guarantee that your GVPS already knows where it is, right at this very moment.

Fulfillment

Some people say that money can't buy happiness. However, I disagree!

Money is indeed a major factor in day-to-day happiness. It's difficult to feel happy when your basic needs aren't being meet. We all require enough money for food, shelter, clothing, and a few of life's little luxuries (such as a *reasonable* amount of throw pillows). Let's face it, if you give a homeless person some food and a place to live, most likely he or she will feel happier.

However, during my quest for simplicity, I learned something quite surprising about the nature of happiness: at some point, spending *more money* did not buy me *more happiness*.

The famous director, Tom Shadyac, has a very similar story. In his documentary I AM, he describes his personal journey to fame and fortune and his "Aha!" moment when he realized that having more wealth was not synonymous with feeling more fulfilled. As a result, Tom urges us to "redefine what it means to be happy." The renowned actor Jim Carrey also arrived at a similar conclusion: "I think everybody should get rich and famous . . . so they can see that it's not the answer."

In my case, I had to admit that buying a different shade of foundation, a new dress, or another fluffy pillow didn't make me any happier. Paying for an infrequently used guest room didn't cure my feelings of loneliness. None of my gazingus pins provided any sort of lasting joy. Even though indulging in a bit of retail therapy made me feel happier in the moment, my shopping induced "high" was always short-lived.

In fact, spending more money often *detracted* from my sense of well-being. When I had a bigger house, I had to spend more time maintaining it. When I owned more stuff, I had a harder time finding the things I actually needed. When I purchased yet another gazingus pin, my temporary feelings of fulfillment were quickly mitigated by the stress I felt when my credit card bill arrived.

Hence, my quest for simplicity resulted in a profound awareness:

I was looking for love in all the wrong places.

This realization made a big difference in my financial bottom line. When I finally stopped looking for love in a new outfit, a bottle of foundation, or another ivory throw pillow, I saved a lot of money.

So, here's what I'm getting at. If we feel lonely, isolated, disconnected, underappreciated, or even bored, does buying something actually make us feel better? Although the "shopper's high" may soothe our troubled soul in the moment, it's just a temporary "fix." We can't avoid the true cause of our discontent forever (unless we want to remain spiritual and broke). Furthermore, if we spend money on yet another gazingus pin, we also make our financial situation worse, which just adds to our stress and negativity. It's a vicious cycle!

So, how do we conquer our gazingus pins?

Here's a very simple technique that I use. Before I pull out my credit card or plunk down my hard-earned cash, I pause for a moment and ask myself a simple yet essential question:

Am I buying something that I love or am I trying to buy love?

Every place is the wrong place to look for love other than WITHIN, where it is really generated from.
ABRAHAM HICKS

AM I WORTHY?

"Your need for acceptance can make you invisible in this world. Don't let anything stand in the way of the light that shines through this form. Risk being seen in all of your glory."

JIM CARREY

That's All Fine and Dandy, But . . .

The magic of simplicity is a powerful tool. The benefits of eliminating the clutter extend way beyond the joy of having a clean closet or well-organized sock drawer; it actually helps us uncover our "hidden treasures"—the unconscious spending habits that fail to produce lasting joy or value in our lives. Addressing our unrewarding spending patterns is paramount to turning our finances around.

Nevertheless, didn't I overlook one very important issue? Sure, the magic of simplicity is all fine and dandy, but what if your lifestyle is incredibly frugal *already* and you're *still* spiritual and broke? What if you simply don't make very much money?

I used to believe that the best way to generate more money was to work harder. Like many of us, I worked an insane number of hours, sometimes sacrificing my health and relationships in the process. My employees accurately described me as a workaholic. Hence, when I was spiritual and broke, I was also *spiritual and exhausted!*

Can you relate?

Now that I've turned my finances around, I can attest to the fact that sacrificing our emotional and physical well-being to create financial wealth isn't the answer. How can we truly feel abundant if our revenue is the product of pain and suffering? As the politician Paul Tsongas said, "No man ever said on his deathbed I wish I had spent more time in the office!" Even if we are living our purpose and love what we do, we can't neglect the importance of creating balance in our lives.

So, if working ourselves to death doesn't work, what's the answer?

As we discussed before, our bank account balance is a reflection of the abundance within us (rather than just the number of hours we work). In other words, we have the uncanny and magical ability to *attract* or *repel* money based on the energy we project into the world. Like water rushing down a stream, money has the capacity and *inclination* to flow to us easily and effortlessly. Unfortunately, many of us are very skilled at creating well-built dams, essentially blocking the flow of abundance in our life.

I used to be very good at building my own financial barricades as well. In fact, I spent over five years working with an exceptional business coach to understand *how* I was getting in the way of my own financial flow. Based on everything I learned during this time, I believe that there is one core issue or "energy block" that prevents us from generating a healthy and happy stream of revenue. In this chapter, we examine what this block is and how to move past it.

Let me begin by telling a story . . .

Patches

Once upon a time, there was a beautiful white-and-black cat named Patches. Sadly, she was a stray kitty, and like many homeless cats, she lived a difficult life on the street, always on the prowl for her next meal or a warm place to sleep. Despite her dismal living conditions, Patches had a dream. She often fantasized about sailing to the enchanted island of Catopia and making it her new home. According to the legend of Catopia, the fortuitous residents of this feline Utopia enjoy an endless supply of kitty treats, cuddles, and warm places to sleep. No kitty is ever left behind!

Fueled by visions of a happier life, Patches secured a job rehabilitating traumatized mice and saved as much money as she could. In the evenings and weekends, she studied how other felines triumphantly completed the arduous journey to Catopia. She spent countless hours researching how to sail, who the best guides were, what supplies to bring, and the optimal time of year to begin the journey.

Finally, after a year of diligent preparation, Patches eagerly set sail for the island of Catopia. She felt excited about the new life ahead of her and incredibly proud of herself for finally pursuing her dream.

However, little did she know that danger lurked ahead . . .

Shortly into her journey, she encountered a severely disturbed dragon named Block. Although Block didn't breathe fire, his cruel words were nearly just as fatal: "Patches, you would be the most incredible cat in Catopia, if only you didn't have that black spot around your eye. It's such a shame!" Regrettably, Block struck a nerve. Patches had always felt self-conscious about her black spot, and now Block had just reinforced her worst

judgment about herself. She took the evil dragon's words
to heart, questioning whether she deserved a happy
life on Catopia. She immediately stopped the boat and
decided to focus instead on slaying her own personal
dragon—that dreaded black spot.

Patches tried many things to get rid of her so-called
"flaw," including surgery, workshops, acupuncture,
catnip, crystals, and energy healing. She spent hours on
the phone with other sympathetic cats lamenting about
her horrible black spot. Sometimes she felt too upset to
eat and would stay in bed all day feeling sorry for herself.
She often blamed her black spot for ruining her life.

One day Patches felt more depressed than ever. On the
verge of giving up, she bowed her head, begging God one
last time: "Please, please remove my black spot so that
I can be happy." With tears in her eyes, she finished her
desperate prayer and looked up. Suddenly she noticed a
bright light appear before her. The glowing orb started to
swirl, vibrate, and become larger and larger. "What was
that?" she wondered with trepidation.

Patches watched in awe as a gorgeous white cat with
magnificent silver wings emerged from the light. The
angelic feline dusted off her fur and introduced herself.
"Good afternoon! I'm your Fairy Catmother, Agnus Dei
(or just Agnus to my friends). I have come to help you."
Agnus paused for a moment, looked deeply into Patches'
eyes, and said, "I have heard your prayers and have
an urgent message for you. You have a very important

decision to make. If you spend any more time focusing on your black spot, you will *never* make it to Catopia."

At first Patches felt outraged by her Fairy Catmother's dire words of warning. She meowed in despair and desperation, "Why me? I'm ugly! Everywhere I go, I feel embarrassed by my black spot. Don't you understand? I can't bear to show my face on Catopia. Even if I do make it, other cats will make fun of me! So why bother?"

Agnus couldn't bear the thought of Patches giving up on her dream. If only Patches could recognize how precious she truly was! With great love and compassion, Agnus said, "Patches, you worked long and hard to prepare for your journey; you hired the best guides; you saved money; you gathered plenty of supplies. You were doing so well! You've already accomplished everything you need to do to achieve your dream. The only problem right now is that you're focusing on the black spot instead of putting your energy into what you truly want!"

And with that, Agnus was gone.

With a jolt, Patches woke up from her horrible nightmare of self-deprecation. She realized that her Fairy Catmother was right. Patches cried out, "Agnus, if you can still hear me, I finally get it! I can still reach Catopia, even if the black spot comes with me." Intense determination filled her eyes, as Patches hoisted her sails and set off again for the island of Catopia.

At long last, Patches arrived on the enchanted island and lived happily ever after, basking in the sun and enjoying *exactly* five belly rubs per day. Ironically, the Queen of Catopia adored the unique and unusual beauty of Patches' black spot. Although she intended to treat all of the Catopia residents equally, she couldn't help but give Patches a few extra kitty treats from time to time. Patches was indeed a very special cat.

Black Spots

Like Patches, many of us possess our own black spots. While we may not have a dark patch of fur around our eye, many of us possess personal attributes that we harshly judge, vehemently dislike, or don't want to face. As a result, we tell ourselves self-destructive, antagonistic, and disheartening stories, such as:

I have nothing to offer the world (or my clients, or employer).
My book (healing modality, artwork, music, webinar, etc.) sucks.
I'll never be as successful as Elizabeth Gilbert.
I'm a loser because I can't afford a house.
I feel worthless.
I'm too depressed to get out of bed.
I'm an ineffective business owner.
I'm a lousy speaker.
I've made too many mistakes.
I'm too fat.

Any of this sound familiar?

Regrettably, our black spots tend to interfere with our ability to attract abundance and achieve our dreams. Instead of focusing on our goals, we spend our precious resources and time trying to fix our black spots. Maybe we go to workshop after workshop, visit numerous plastic surgeons, spend hours complaining to our friends, indulge in retail therapy, or eat too much chocolate as a way to compensate for our so-called "flaws." Thus, we sabotage our success by living in the land of "if only": If only I were ten pounds lighter, or famous, or had more money, or owned a house, or had more Instagram followers, or was married to a wonderful spouse, or . . . *then (and only then)* would I be worthy of what I truly want.

This tendency to focus on our black spots is the core issue that prevents us from creating financial abundance. Like a chameleon, this energy block takes many forms, such as procrastination, undercharging for our services, hesitancy to market our practice, lack of perseverance, and the list goes on and on.

The Underpaid

Many healing practitioners have shared with me that they don't feel comfortable charging money for their services. (This might explain why they struggle to make ends meet!) Healing practitioners aren't the only ones with this troublesome mindset. Employees wrestle with the idea of asking for a raise, let alone actually doing it; spiritual business owners feel guilty at the mere thought of increasing their prices; artists sell their work for a lot less than it's worth. Over and over again, I have run across people who are doing what they love yet are "underpaid." Although they work hard, they simply do not receive what they deserve for their time and experience.

When I ask people, "Why are you hesitant to ask for more money?" the most common justification I receive goes something like this: "My life isn't perfect (I'm not married, beautiful, young, healthy, or wealthy), so I don't feel like I have much to offer my clients (or my boss, or my customers)."

In my case, I was extremely hesitant to charge enough money to cover our expenses for our Quantum-Touch products and services. I felt even more uncomfortable (and sometimes still do) with the concept of making a profit. In fact, like many small, heart-centered businesses, we were undercharging to the point where we were threatening our own survival. My tendency to charge too little combined with my propensity to overspend was a lethal combination. I'm surprised we never filed for bankruptcy!

Like many healers, when I thought about raising my prices, I felt very uneasy, telling myself, "If you raise prices, people won't like you anymore," or "If you are truly serving others, you need to keep your fees low." I desperately craved approval from others and was afraid of "rocking the boat." Because I didn't think I "was good enough," I was spending a lot of time, constantly trying to people-please.

In essence, I was making a common yet crucial mistake: I allowed my black spots to make my pricing decisions. As I'm sure you have figured out by now, listening to our black spots tends to keep us spiritual and broke!

Priceless

Black spots are notorious for offering bad advice. When it comes to establishing our fees or asking for a raise, our black spots will be all too happy to chime in with their misguided and destructive opinions, telling us fear-based stories, such as:

Your fee is way too high.
You're crazy to charge that much.
No one will ever pay that much.
If you charge that amount, you will lose clients, friends, customers, your job, or business.
You don't deserve a raise.
You can only charge that much after you lose ten pounds
(or get married or have a degree or have a net worth of over $1,000,000.)

In essence, our black spots urge us to ask for as little as possible, insisting that we're unworthy or incompetent. Yet what our black spots fail to understand—and this is important—is that there is a huge difference between *proving worth* and *providing value*. Black spots will insist that our goal in life is to show the world how important we are—to seek outside validation for our worthiness as human beings. Instead, though, our life purpose revolves around helping others, not justifying our significance.

Imagine that you write a book that changes someone's life. Or through your coaching practice, you save a marriage. Or your art brings immense joy and appreciation to someone's life. Or with your healing work, one of your clients overcomes cancer.

Seeing the life-changing value of our work is wonderfully gratifying, isn't it?

While running Quantum-Touch, I have experienced the immense satisfaction that comes from making a profound impact on the lives of other people. We have consistently seen that Quantum-Touch is really effective for pain relief. Countless customers have experienced a significant reduction in pain using our modality, even after trying everything else. Sometimes Quantum-Touch was the *only* technique that dissipated their pain after years and years of misery.

So, what is the value of getting rid of pain?

Let's face it, when you are in severe pain, nothing else matters, right? Lots of chronic pain sufferers would pay almost *anything* for even just a brief respite from their pain. Some would argue that pain relief is more important than all the money in the world.

Some would even suggest that the value of healing their pain is *priceless*.

So, here's what I'm getting at. When we do what we love,

we are offering our love to the world. In return, the people that we touch receive a priceless gift. Hence, contrary to what our black spots might suggest, money is simply a tool that enables us to *fund our life mission*—not a reflection of our self-worth. In other words, financial alignment empowers us to provide more value to more people—which is priceless, by the way!

Speaking of priceless, let's talk about free love.

Free Love

I've encountered so many people who believe that they must give away their work for free to be "spiritual" or "loving." I call this belief the "free love argument," and it sounds something like:

"Well, all healing energy comes from God, so I can't charge money for it."

This might surprise you, but I believe that the "free love argument" is actually a black spot in disguise. If you feel that being "spiritual" means giving away your work for free, what you are really saying that God/Goddess/All That Is/Source is providing all the value (not you). Your black spot is using God as an excuse to convince you of your unworthiness.

See how tricky these black spots are?

Even if God or Spirit *does* do all the work through you, you are still facilitating the session; you are still providing value to the client.

Imagine if we applied this free love argument to the produce at the supermarket. Apples and oranges grow on trees, all on their own; they are a gift from God. If we had our own apple orchid, we could eat all the apples we could ever want "for free." Hence, when we buy produce at the store, what then are we paying for? If it's a gift from God, shouldn't all of the produce be free?

Of course not!

Someone had to buy the land, plant the apple orchid, pick the produce at the right time, package it up, deliver it to the store, and pay their taxes.

Let's take this one step further. I believe that part of the value we offer to our clients and customers is the fee that we charge. For example, at Quantum-Touch, we teach energy healing workshops around the world and we charge what we consider a balanced fee for our two-day workshops. Occasionally, when we have given away free workshops, I've noticed something fascinating about our nonpaying students. Compared to those who paid the full fee, our "free love" recipients generally tend to show up late (if they show up at all), study their phones during the workshops, appear less engaged, and are generally less committed to learning Quantum-Touch. They do not appreciate the value. When people pay the full workshop fee, they show up on time, take notes, and are very dedicated to learning the modality; they are invested in the process.

Charging a fee not only allows us to do what we love, it also creates the space for our client or customer to fully commit to what they love!

The Two-Star Review

Would you like to know the formula for keeping everyone happy?
Simple . . . there isn't any.
AUTHOR UNKNOWN

When I launched my first book, *Love Incorporated*, in 2016, I quickly learned that not everyone loved my book. Although I received a lot of positive feedback, I felt terribly disturbed when I saw my first "critical" two-star review on Amazon. (If you're not familiar with the Amazon review process, Amazon allows readers to rate a book by giving it one to five stars, with five being the highest. A two-star review is the equivalent of getting a D in school!)

Although I had plenty of five-star reviews, the discouraging feedback from my unhappy reader sent me into a spiral of negativity, narrated by my rather prolific inner critic:

Geez, this reader is right; I totally suck.
Most writers are way better than me.
Why did I even bother to write a book in the first place?
What was I thinking?
Maybe I should give up writing.
I'd be a much better writer if only I were ten pounds lighter
(just kidding!)

My unfavorable Amazon review quickly inspired my "author-specific" black spots to rise to the surface. I seriously questioned my worth as a writer—briefly forgetting that my life's purpose is about providing value, not proving worth.

In a misguided attempt to sooth my feelings of dejection, I browsed the Amazon reviews of one of my favorite authors, Elizabeth Gilbert. Her book, *Eat Pray Love*, sold over ten million copies worldwide and later became a mainstream movie. *Time Magazine* called her one of the one hundred most influential people in the world. To me, she represents the epitome of an incredibly successful author.

So, you can imagine my surprise when I saw that *Eat Pray Love* had over *1,400 critical reviews*! Some people even made their negative commentary personal, describing her book as an "autobiography about a needy, self-centered person." Wow! Really? I took great comfort in the fact that even Elizabeth Gilbert was not immune to the negative review.

Nevertheless, the significant adverse impact of my unfavorable review led me to wonder:

Why do we feel so hurt by the criticism of others?

I believe that we are vulnerable to critical reviews when we obstinately entertain the painful idea that they might actually be true. The judgment of others disturbs us *only* when they reinforce our own destructive and antagonistic beliefs about ourselves. For example, if someone suggests that I have bizarre purple feathers and a strange piglike snout, I would probably either laugh at their comments or quickly run away. However, if someone tells me that I'm chubby, I'm more likely to feel upset because I've always felt self-conscious about my weight. Even without any encouragement from outside criticism, sometimes our black spots rear their ugly heads all by themselves. Often my pessimistic and condemning self-assessment has resulted in my own self-created two-star review.

Our black spots can be strangely mesmerizing and incredibly compelling, absorbing our precious time and energy like a drama-filled, demoralizing, dysfunctional relationship. Sometimes, they chip away at our well-being for years, or even decades. However, despite their tenacity, many of us rarely question whether or not our black spots are actually true.

For example, one of my most distressing childhood memories occurred when I was in fourth grade at my weekly gymnastics class. While eagerly awaiting my turn to practice my tumbling, I was in my happy place. Sadly, my vivacity quickly turned to vexation with just a few thoughtless words from my coach. She said, "Your belly is really hanging out."

Did she just say I was too fat?

She did!

Worse yet, I believed her! I felt incredibly hurt and ashamed.

With intense determination to never to be called "fat" again, I started my first diet when I was nine years old. Although I quickly lost a few pounds, I never lost touch with the hurtful sting of those words; they have haunted me throughout my adult life, even now, almost forty years later. I must admit, I'm still guilty of telling myself various versions of the "I'm too fat" story on a regular basis:

I'm too fat to be a public speaker.
I look chubby in my photos.
I'm too fat for a relationship.

In fact, I would often recite these self-depreciating stories without ever questioning my own critical review.

Is it true?

Am I really too fat?

Well, let's see...

Compared to an ultra-thin supermodel, I am too fat for the cover of *Vogue* (and not tall enough either). A doctor would say that I'm well within the normal weight for my height. If I had been alive during the Renaissance, I would have been considered not fat enough.

So again, am I too fat?

It's really a matter of perspective.

Our two-star reviews, whether they are self-generated or originate from others, are just a particular frame of reference, completely and altogether relative. Our black spots are merely a product of our own nonfactual, idiosyncratic, prejudiced, and judgmental frame of reference.

Speaking of relativity, the negative critiques of *Eat Pray Love* are merely sparsely interspersed among a vast collection of positive reviews, not unlike a few errant notes in a perfectly executed symphony. The majority of readers gave

Gilbert's book glowing reviews, calling it "life-changing," "outstanding," and "transcendent."

So, here's what I'm getting at. Like Patches, we have a choice. Do we take our judgments to heart, wallow in them, and splash around in the negativity like a gleeful pig in the mud? Or do we dust off our wings, stop listening to the critics (ourselves included!) and continue to follow our heart?

"How others treat me is their path;
how I react is mine."

WAYNE DYER

The Ghosts Within

"Monsters are real; ghosts are real too. They live inside us,
and sometimes they win."
STEPHEN KING

Black spots are pesky, disruptive, parasitic creatures. Many of us find them difficult to eradicate. They can be more tenacious than a horde of persistent ants marching toward a sugar-laden treat. And if you do manage to get rid of one, another one seems all too eager to take its place.

Throughout my life I have struggled with a multitude of these nettlesome black spots, including one very tenacious and self-punishing black spot called "I'm too fat." I've devoted a lot of time and energy to this particular black spot—trying crazy diets, going hungry, enduring twice-daily weigh-ins, and spending countless hours at the gym.

After years of struggling with my "I'm too fat" critical review, I noticed a peculiar phenomenon about this particular black spot. No matter how much I weighed, what size I wore, or what others said, I would still identify with this "I'm too fat" story. My black spot was much more than a spot; it was a voracious black hole that could never be filled. It was an ever-present excuse to wallow in self-loathing.

Wanting to lose weight is not necessarily a bad thing. Having a vision, pursuing a dream, and following your heart is always worth striving for! Nothing was wrong with my desire to sculpt my body into what I considered the "ideal human form." The real problem was my insistent focus on my critical reviews and my internal contempt.

Instead of doing the work to make my goals happen, I would do battle with my black spots, often spending my day wallowing in depression, feeling sorry for myself, or worse yet, buying more gazingus pins. Hence, I was investing in my black spot rather than devoting my sacred energy to actually pursuing my dreams.

My black spots ran my life. I gave them permission to sabotage my success and make my decisions for me. They told me how to spend my time and where to focus my energy. They gave me bad advice about money. They distracted me, mocked me, and caused me to veer off course from my heart and Divine Guidance. They were the ghosts within, endlessly haunting me with their pessimistic voices.

So, how do we eradiate these black spots?

The answer is, "We don't!" Remember my story about

performing on the flying trapeze? I constantly chastised myself for my fear of heights, until my trapeze instructor offered me the advice that completely changed my relationship with fear: "The goal of trapeze is not to eliminate fear but to be operational with the fear present." After that, I felt liberated. I no longer felt obligated to fight my fears; I made peace with them instead.

This same philosophy works equally well with black spots. Instead of focusing on a black spot, trying to eliminate it, or giving it our precious time and energy, we simply embrace the pesky little creature. We can accept our black spots, without identifying with them or allowing them to derail our whole journey. We embrace our black spots with just one caveat: At no time does any black spot have the authority to make decisions for us. They can come along for the ride, but under no circumstances are they allowed to drive!

So, let's make friends with our black spots, thank them for showing up in all their glory, and then joyfully continue doing what we love!

Talk to yourself like you would talk to someone you love.
OPRAH WINFREY

SPIRITUAL AND ABUNDANT

*Money at its very essence is energy and
all energy can be attracted or repelled.*

AUTHOR UNKNOWN

Why Do Bad Things Happen to Good People?

If Life Is a Bowl of Cherries, What Am I Doing in the Pits? I'm sure we all can relate to this quirky and sarcastic title of the well-known book by Erma Bombeck, an incredibly popular humorist in the 1980s. With a series of best-selling books and weekly columns syndicated by nine hundred newspapers, she was well-loved by millions. Ironically, she had suffered from polycystic kidney disease her entire life and then, at the age of sixty-nine, she *finally* received a kidney transplant, only to die a few weeks later from complications due to the operation.

Tragic, right?

Speaking of tragic irony, Bombeck's story reminds me of the 1970's American rock band Lynyrd Skynyrd. In 1977, at the peak of their success, a plane crash took the lives of three band members. The accident happened just three days after the release of *Street Survivors*, which became an instant hit, achieving gold record status in just ten days. What strikes me as *particularly* ironic is that the original cover art for *Street Survivors* depicted a photograph of the band standing on a city street, engulfed in flames. (Out of respect for the deceased, MCA Records withdrew the original cover.)

Stories like these tend to make me wonder, *What the heck was the Universe thinking?* Haven't we all pondered the strange, paradoxical, and mysterious mind of God (or Spirit/the Universe/All That Is) at some point?

Why did God allow this to happen?
Why do I have to suffer?

When it seems like we're living "in the pits," it's only natural to wonder, "Why me?" For many of us, this issue often lies at the forefront of our hearts and minds during times of intense tragedy and despair. Likewise, it's woven throughout the tapestry of this entire book—the common, holographic thread that ties everything together. In fact, right from the start, we raised this very question—a poignant, difficult, and oftentimes heartbreaking question that for many of us is all too painfully familiar: Have you ever had a moment in your life that was so shocking, so horrible, and yet appeared so absurdly random, that you were compelled to wonder:

"How the heck did I end up here?"

I pondered this perplexing and disturbing question as I numbly watched the sunrise from the back of a police car, after that horrible sexual assault and robbery. Again, I asked this same bewildering question whenever I contemplated the pitiful state of my financial affairs. I was convinced that some unseen and malevolent force was working against me, bound and determined to keep me spiritual and broke. Consequently, I spent *a lot* of time feeling sorry for myself, unappreciated, and angry at the Universe.

After my sexual assault, I felt *especially* sorry for myself. I didn't understand how the *heck* I ended up here: exhausted, traumatized, and broke, not only financially but emotionally as well. I desperately needed some way to make sense of all the seemingly senseless tragedies in the world. So, fueled by my anger, sorrow, confusion, and lack of sleep, I embarked on a healing quest, bound and determined to find an answer, *once and for all,* to the age-old question:

Why do bad things happen to good people?

My journey took many twists and turns, and after five years of intense soul-searching, I finally had my answer.

As it turned out, I was asking the *wrong* question!

The famous psychiatrist Carl Jung remarked, "To ask the right question is already half the solution of a problem." Apparently, wondering "why me" while wallowing around in self-pity wasn't the most productive way to understand how the Universe works! Contrary to what I used to believe, there are no "random acts of evil;" bad things don't just "happen" to good people; and I didn't just haphazardly "end up" as the victim of a sexual assault. Likewise, my money problems weren't the result of "bad luck," taxes, an economic downturn, or the whim of an arbitrary God.

Rather, the Universe was simply responding to my vibration.

According to the Law of Attraction, the Universe functions like a giant mirror that reflects back to us exactly what we project onto it. If we manifest certain experiences into our lives, it's because, on some level, we are an energetic match to them. In other words, *like attracts like.* If we're carrying around a lot of anger, for example, we will attract more things to be angry about. If we absolutely love kittens, we'll attract more kittens into our lives! (This actually happened in my own life. At one point, I was caring for nine kittens, none of which came from a shelter; all of them found their way to my doorstep!)

Although life may *seem* unfair, the Law of Attraction is just as impartial as the law of gravity. The Universe is pure love; it does not judge; it does not reward "good" people and "punish" the "bad." Rather, we *create* our *entire* reality (no exceptions). The Universe cannot defy our vibration.

Hence, instead of asking "How the heck did I end up here?" I invite us all to ponder a different question:

a brave question;

a scary question;

a controversial question even.

What within me attracted my experience?

Once we see the entire world as a reflection of who we are, we then have the power to actually make a change. As we discussed before, our world is like a giant box of LEGOs, with one exception: instead of plastic, these special LEGOs are composed entirely of *energy*. We can use these energetic building blocks to carefully craft our ideal world—or create a horrible mess.

It's entirely up to us!

This explains why doing what we love doesn't *automatically* attract abundance into our lives. If our vibration is not aligned with financial prosperity, then it's *impossible* to create abundance *no matter what we do*. This also explains why cutting up our credit cards isn't always the most productive way to reduce our spending!

Spiritual and Abundant

The only way we can change the repetitive patterns in our lives is to *rework our own energetic patterns within*. If we want to increase our bank account balance, get out of debt (or even manifest lots of kittens), we need to shift our own vibration so that we're an energetic match for what we want.

Throughout this book, I have provided some simple yet powerful tools to change our energy around money. I've used these techniques myself, and my net worth went from horribly negative to comfortably positive in a relatively short period of time. I paid off all my debt, saved a bunch of money, and no longer feel stressed about money.

And believe me, if I can do it, *anyone* can!

So, here's what I'm getting at: The secret to prosperity lies within our own heart. It goes beyond creating a career doing what we love—although that's a great start! It's about approaching every aspect of our lives, every decision, every crisis, every purchase, and even every moment of our day with our heart fully open. It's about living in alignment with our heart. In essence, we create abundance when we lead with our heart—when the inspiration and motivation behind every choice we make is love (rather than fear, scarcity, victimhood, anger, sadness, unworthiness, self-judgment, etc.).

Are we a martyr for the cause? Or do we love living our purpose?

Are we listening to the random chatter of the mind? Or are we following our Divine Guidance?

Do we love where we live? Or do we live where we think we *should*?

Are we investing our energy (financial or otherwise) in what we truly love? Or are we trying to buy love?

Are we trying to prove our worth or provide value?

Are we focusing on our black spots? Or are we living the life of our dreams?

Are we connected to our heart?

And here's the final irony I'll leave you with: prosperity is not about money at all! Our whole life is a treasure hunt to find our own inner abundance, the love within us.

So, yes, there is a mysterious and unseen Force that shapes our lives. It can be a source of misery and despair or a source or great joy, gratitude, and happiness. It can keep us spiritual and broke or empower us to create a life that is both spiritual *and* abundant.

We are that Force.

ACKNOWLEDGMENTS

Writing a book is primarily a solitary activity, which means spending a lot of time alone in front of a computer, eating chocolate and pondering the best way to say something (and then promptly deleting it and writing it again!). However, despite the solitary nature of writing, I was lucky enough to be surrounded by some amazing people during the process of creating *Spiritual and Broke*.

First of all, this book may never have happened if it weren't for my amazing friend and coach Leigh St. John. Over the last two years, she has encouraged me to be the best writer I can, reviewing every line of prose in painstaking detail, and providing essential, astute, and honest feedback. I couldn't have done it without her!

To Richard Gordon, my dear friend and business partner of over sixteen years, who displayed great optimism and creativity during times where we were desperately spiritual and broke. I am immensely grateful you have been such an amazing part of my life.

To all the wonderful, heart-centered people in the Quantum-Touch community—especially our instructors, employees, and practitioners. Thank you for sharing your love and light with the world.

To James "Mac" McMinn, my dear friend, thank you for opening my eyes to the possibility of a world without financial struggles, leading by example in your own life. You have been a wonderful source of encouragement, and love.

To my dear friend and fellow writer Stefan Malecek, who was one of the first people that read this book! I appreciate his wise counsel, encouragement, and long talks about life, the Universe, and Everything.

To all the wonderful people at Union Square Publishing who were willing to take on a new author. Thank you for giving this book a chance.

Finally, to all the wonderful cats and kittens who have graced my life, providing endless cuddles and a unique perspective on life. Thank you Patches, Sam, Lilly, Violet, Rainbow, Nemo, Mango, Enzo, Devi, Fushi, and Linus.

Love and Light,
Jennifer Noel Taylor

ABOUT THE AUTHOR

Jennifer Noel Taylor has always believed that the Universe is full of magic and miracles.

After graduating from Cal Poly (San Luis Obispo, California) with a bachelor of science degree in Computer Science and a minor in Philosophy, Jennifer started her first job as a software engineer at a large company in San Diego. Although her job paid the bills, it didn't align with her true passion in life. To cope with the disillusion she felt with work, she studied bodywork and energy healing in her free time. After attending the International Professional School of Bodywork, Esalen Institute in Big Sur, and the Maui Academy of Healing Arts, Jennifer received a *very clear intuitive* message that energy healing was her true calling in life. So, she took a leap of faith, left the software industry, and made the field of energy healing her new career. Since 2002, she has been the CEO (or "Chief Magical Officer," as she likes to call it) of Quantum-Touch, Inc.

As the Chief Magical Officer of Quantum-Touch, Jennifer continues to promote optimal wellness by helping people connect more deeply to their love. Her business practices include spiritually rewarding jobs, loving service to the world, environmental responsibility, and financial abundance. She grew Quantum-Touch from a regional U.S company to a multinational corporation. Jennifer currently lives on Maui, loves to volunteer for the Humane Society, and fosters kittens.

"Imagine...If more people did what they love,
how much more joyful the world would be."
JENNIFER NOEL TAYLOR

9 781946 928221